From Holocaust to Hallelujah

DEDICATION
To my mother Hilda Lewin. Without her many selfless sacrifices, I would not have lived.

From Holocaust to Hallelujah

by Dieter "Dan" Lewin
as told to Keith Wilkerson

Champions Unlimited
PUBLISHERS

Copyright © 2007 by Dieter "Dan" Lewin

All rights reserved. No part of this book may be reproduced without permission from the publisher, except by a reviewer who may quote brief passages in a review, nor may any part of this book be reproduced, stored in a retrieval system or copied by mechanical photocopying, recording or other mean without permission from the publisher.

Author's Note: No pictures of me as a child survived our escape from Schloppe or the multiple times our family lost everything in the bombings of Berlin. So, the photos on the cover are of other Jewish children during the same period, all believed to have been taken by Nazi photographers.

The children behind the barbed wire on the front cover are believed to have died in Auschwitz's gas chambers shortly after the photo was taken. On the back cover, a Jewish mother bids her little boy goodbye forever shortly after he was separated out to be killed with others too small to work.

The boy with his hands uplifted was captured in Warsaw. At least two survivors have come forward who say they believe the picture was taken of them.

My thanks and apreciation go out to Bryan Gaskill for the book title and to Pat Gladden for helping with editing.

I would like to express my deep appreciation to the many organizations which are hurrying to preserve the personal stories of the last surviving victims of the Nazi reign of terror, we, the legendary "hidden children" of the Holocaust.

We are the final witnesses of the horror. I was there.
I saw it all.

ISBN: 978-0-9799253-0-6

Champions Unlimited, Publishers

P.O. Box 185, Berryville, AR 72616 USA

Write to us at christcrew@aol.com

Published in the United States of America

Foreword

For those the Father foreknew, He also predestined.
Romans 8:29

As a five-year-old Jew hiding from roving teenage Hitler Youth gangs, I didn't know what predestination means. I certainly never gave it any thought as I obeyed my older friends and did not move, did not cry out – did not give our hiding place away.

I certainly didn't see it as I cowered on Berlin's streetcars, staring mutely as fascist Brown Shirts beat elderly Jews and as my mother quietly whispered to me not to look, not to protest, not to try to help them.

As my grandfather, the rabbi of the little town of Schloppe, Germany, was dragged away in front of my eyes to a death camp, I did not see the Almighty's hand in what was happening.

But as six million other Jews across Europe were systematically murdered, I was miraculously spared.

Why me? Looking back now, I can see how our Creator guided my life from birth.

He molded my character and equipped me to be of service to Him. We all have the tendency to say, "Why me, Lord?" or "Why do all these things happen to me?"

It may be too easy to say that if we live our lives the best we can and do not knowingly reject His gentle leading, He in turn will faithfully craft a beautiful quilt for us.

The very idea that a loving Father had His hand on me was a hard lesson for me to learn. But now looking back, it all makes sense.

I came through the fire.

I have hidden in the valleys of the shadow of death. I have hungered, even starved, in the presence of my enemies.

I did not pray.

The Almighty Creator of the Universe was just an abstraction to me – a tradition. I did not look to Him for help. I did not see His mighty hand in anything.

But today I know that His handiwork can easily be seen everywhere – in nature, in daily events and even on the darkest road. It is on that roadway our character is formed. It is in that fire that we are refined and transformed.

It takes a concentrated effort on our part – far greater than even Hitler – to upset His creation. We cannot see the future. We rarely understand the Father's leading. There are times when we think our lives are not going well – in fact, when we wonder how things could get any worse.

I know. *I lived through it.*

I certainly did not see anything of beauty as British and American bombers filled the skies, raining fire and destruction on both Nazi and Jew, on military targets as well as civilian homes – as Nazi Germany was pounded into submission.

Beaten, kicked and left crying on the sidewalk by Hitler Youth hooligans, it certainly never occurred to me as a little boy that as we live our lives, we can walk in the Father's perfect plan or through our will we can force our way and do it our own way.

Surviving the daily emptiness of having my playmates disappear without a trace, I did not see the hand of any Creator.

Today, I know that He has every step marked out for our good. By His grace, I survived. But it took me a long time to understand who He is – and why He permitted this terrible nightmare.

I would like to share the meanings of the patches in my life's quilt with you, in the hope that you will be able to look back at your life and see the Father's hand in your life as well.

I learned that trusting Him is the only way. He has a plan. *Even if we cannot see it.*

His plan for us is a beautiful quilt with each piece fitted masterfully into its perfect place.

We have the tendency to want to create our own patches and fit them into the quilt. I believe we can alter or delay His perfect plan through our stubbornness. Sometimes, He has to let us walk in what we created to bring us back to His perfection.

This might cause us pain and hardship, but He will gently guide us into the right paths.

So, without my knowledge that He was at work, my wondrous Creator made a beautiful quilt for me.

It did not seem so beautiful at the time.

Chapter One

I remember the terror vividly, although I was just a toddler. Without warning, a big Nazi truck ground to a noisy halt in front of my grandparents' house in a quiet residential neighborhood of Schloppe, Germany.

Enormous stormtroopers in trench coats and black boots, brandishing rifles and pistols, swarmed out of the back and rushed up the walkway. Roughly yelling "Raus, Juden!" – "Get out, Jews!" they pounded on my grandparents' front door with their rifle butts.

From Holocaust to Hallelujah

When my always-calm, friendly, elderly grandfather came to the door, he was grabbed by the beard and thrown to the ground.

I remember.

As my mother hugged me, her hand over my mouth, stifling my cries, the Nazi soldiers kicked him, then shoved him to his feet and rushed him into the street, yelling at him the whole time to run faster, then picking him up and throwing him into the back of the flatbed truck as if he were a bag of garbage.

Yelling and rampaging through the house, they searched for anybody else and began throwing furniture through the glass windows. We heard cries of protest, then terrified screams as they dragged my dignified, weeping grandmother out into the street, then dumped her into the truck and drove away.

And the street filled with silent neighbors was quiet. Every face turned to us.

I was only two years old, but to this day the scene remains clear in my mind. Embedded in my memory is my mother's face, terrified as she stood silently accused by the unspeaking crowd.

Down the street, the soldiers stopped again – this time at our house. From the back of the truck, terrified, indignant, weeping Jews were calling to us and the neighbors, crying out for someone to help them. The soldiers broke down our door, yelling, "Juden! Schnell raus!" ("Jews! Out quickly!"), then began tearing through our house, searching for us.

But my mother and I were not home. We were watching from the street.

My mother hid my face, holding me tightly to her as the soldiers rampaged through our home, yelling, breaking things, throwing furniture and calling out for my father to surrender himself.

I remember how the neighbors silently stared at us, but said nothing as the truck went on down the street in search of my Uncle Max and my godparents, the Gotthilfs. But they were gone, having sold what they could only weeks before and sailing to America.

The stormtroopers herded all of Schloppe's Jews – all but me and my father (my mother was Catholic) – from their homes, prodding them like cattle, laughing as they struck them in the backs and heads with rifle butts, shouting all the time, "Macht schnell, juden!" ("Move quickly, Jew!") – even to the little children. They beat anyone who did not run fast enough, pushing them down the steps and out into the street.

As evening fell, they herded Schloppe's Jews into the center of town.

Even though I was very small, I will never forget the sight of people on the ground,

writhing, blood running from their wounds, kids bigger than me screaming, "Mother, mother ...."
A few had luggage. Most did not. Everywhere, Jews were praying. The stormtroopers turned police dogs on those who knelt. They kicked, hit and shoved everyone toward the marketplace. Shots resounded in the air. One old man in a prayer shawl knelt as a soldier stood behind him with a revolver, taking aim.

I remember one man in particular who had been dragged out of his home wearing only one shoe and no trousers, just his underpants, a suit jacket and a shirt. The soldiers laughed at him, forcing him to march in quickstep, his hands clasped atop his head.

I caught only a glimpse of my grandparents. They dared not look directly at my mother or me for fear of giving us away, managing only terrified glances of goodbye.

Darkness fell and the soldiers drove away with their truck filled with Jews. My mother and I walked home and slipped into our house from the alley. Fearfully, in the dark, she packed quickly – throwing into big suitcases anything of value that hadn't been broken or looted.

She knew it wasn't safe for us to stay. Our

neighbors had not betrayed us yet, but all it would take was one person with a grudge denouncing us to the police.

My father arrived home sometime that night. I remember my hysterical mother falling into his arms after he drove our car into the alley with the headlights off. He had already heard what was happening in other towns – and feared the worst for us.

His parents, my grandparents, had been taken. But my mother and I were safe.

We loaded everything up in the car.

And we fled.

Chapter Two

My mother wept in the front seat, disbelieving what she had seen with her own eyes.

Ninety percent of the German people didn't believe it either. Years later, many would claim not to know what was going on. Nazi propaganda had been very successful in convincing the general public that Jews were hateful and that abusing them showed patriotism – but most Germans didn't attack Jews on the street.

Few knew anything about the

concentration camps where the Jews were herded. After the war, when the book *The Diary of Anne Frank* came out, many Germans exclaimed, "Ah, that's not true! That never happened!"

But it did. I saw it with my own eyes in the autumn of 1938. And I lived the nightmare that followed – the terror that filled the next seven years of my childhood.

Elie Wiesel in his book *Night* writes about what it was like. Frankly, I do not remember many things. I was too little. I believe that I have blotted out many of the terrible things I witnessed.

Wiesel was 12 years old, growing up in the little town of Sighet – old enough to pay attention and know. A scholarly boy, he had enjoyed spending evenings at the synagogue with his grandfatherly mentor, known locally as Moshe the Beadle, since he was the "beadle" or caretaker of the local synagogue.

Old Moshe and 12-year-old Elie would argue long hours into the night about the mysteries of the universe.

Then the government ruled that any Jews unable to prove their citizenship had to be expelled. Elderly Moshe was crammed into a cattle train and sent off to Poland. The people of Sighet wept bitterly as the train left.

However, life returned to normal. Rumors circulated that the deportees had arrived in German-occupied Poland and were working there, satisfied with their new home.

Then somehow Moshe managed to escape, miraculously saved by God, he believed, in order to save the Jews of Sighet. He hurried back to the village to describe what had happened. He ran from one Jewish household to the next.

"Jews, listen to me! It's all I ask of you. No money. No pity. Just listen to me!" he pleaded.

He told how the cattle train crossed the border into Poland, where it was taken over by the Gestapo, the German secret police. The Jews were transferred to trucks and driven to the forest in Galicia, near the town of Kolomaye, where they were forced to dig pits. When they had finished, each prisoner had to stand by the hole, present his neck and was shot.

Babies were thrown into the air and used as targets by machine gunners. Moshe told about Malka, a young girl who took three days to die and Tobias, the tailor, who begged to be killed before his sons. Moshe was shot in the leg and taken for dead.

But the Jews of Sighet would not listen or believe him. "He's just trying to make us pity him. What an imagination he has!" they said.

"Poor fellow. He's gone mad."

In the book Moshe weeps. Young Elie observes how his grandfatherly old friend has changed. He's lost interest in the things he once loved such as God, the mysteries of the Scriptures and singing. He's become entirely consumed with his terrifying stories and tells them to anyone who will listen. But the people of Sighet became weary of his tales, declaring he has lost his mind.

But over the next 18 months, restrictions on the Jews of the little village gradually increase. No valuables can be kept in Jewish homes. Jews are not allowed in restaurants or their own synagogues or away from home after six in the evening. They must wear a yellow star on their clothing at all times.

In the book, time passes and in the spring of 1944, the people of Sighet are certain that Hitler's defeat is imminent. The Allies invade Normandy and the war begins going very badly for the Germans. Elie wants his father to sell everything and to emigrate to Palestine but his father feels he is too old to start a new life.

Then comes the disturbing news that German troops have occupied the town. At first, the soldiers seem friendly as they live peacefully, billeted in private houses. But on the seventh day of Passover, they arrest the leaders of the Jewish community. Jews are not allowed to leave their houses for three days. Then, a Jew no longer has the right to keep gold, jewels or valuables, Elie's father buries their family savings in the basement.

All the Jews are corralled into two small ghettos. Elie and his family already live within the boundaries of the largest one, so they remain in their house, but give up some of their rooms to relatives who have been forced to evacuate.

The Jews then are told the ghettos are being emptied. They are allowed only to take a few personal belongings. The police herd them together, shouting orders to march, then run. To their surprise, the Jews arrive at the other ghetto, which is deserted – the people who were there already have been expelled. Elie goes into his uncle's house only to find a half-finished bowl of soup on the table and a pie waiting to be put in the oven.

Elie's convoy goes to the main synagogue, which has been heavily vandalized and is packed with Jews. They aren't allowed to leave, so they have to relieve themselves in the corners of the building. The next morning they are marched onto waiting cattle wagons. The police cram 80 people into each car. They are given a few loaves of bread and some buckets of water. The windows are barred and the cars sealed. One person is put in charge in each car and told that if anyone escapes, he will be shot.

"Why did we allow ourselves to be taken?" laments Elie. "We could have fled, hidden ourselves in the mountains or in the villages. But we did not know."

Of course, they did know.

Moshe the Beadle had warned them.

But they had refused to believe.

Chapter Three

Shaken by the arrests of his parents and fearful for the safety of our little family, my father obeyed an inspiration that, frankly, made no sense.

Instead of attempting to flee the Nazis by heading for Switzerland or France – or trying to book passage to America, he decided that we would hide in plain sight – in *Berlin!*

I was far too young to know that his plan was outlandish and even foolhardy. But he was convinced that we could disappear into the millions of people thronging into the biggest city in Germany – Berlin, the capital, where Hitler himself lived.

Did my father know the danger into which he was placing me, his young firstborn? In each country overrun by the Nazis, the survival rate of Jewish children was far worse than that of adults.

Nine out of ten Jewish children died, not as a result of some tragic accident or some bureaucratic mistake. *No, it was deliberate.* Such systematic killing of little children is unprecedented in human history. Not even Nero, Stalin or Pol Pot targeted children.

My father could not have known. So, off to Berlin we went.

Many Jewish youngsters who were shipped off to labor camps with their families were killed upon arrival. Others were singled out for gruesome medical experiments – such as exposure to radiation or disease or extreme cold or acids to see how much it would take to cripple them or blind them or kill them.

Most of the Jewish children who survived the Third Reich lived because they were hidden from their persecutors.

Sometimes for years, they lived out of the Nazis' sight, in convents or orphanages, barns or deserted factories or in city sewers beneath the streets.

Some lived openly, concealing their names, pretending not to be Jewish. Only a few lived in the open.

That was my father's plan. We would just go to Berlin and disappear. It was a desperate time. All around us, families were being torn apart. Livelihoods were destroyed. Wealth was looted or confiscated.

People we loved were herded like cattle into filthy slums where they were refused jobs, food or medical care.

We did not know it, but many had already been murdered – often within hours of their arrests. The very old, the very young, the sick and the uncooperative were shot, their bodies dumped into unmarked mass graves.

Some children escaped when their parents were swept up in surprise raids. The terrified children slipped away and were left to fend for themselves. Hiding in slum alleys and abandoned buildings, they came out only at night in search of food and water.

No one knows how many Jewish children like me evaded the Nazis during the war. The only "hidden child" most people have ever heard of is Anne Frank.

But there were many, many more of us, perhaps as many as 100,000, each who lived their own terrible nightmares. Survival depended on wits and personal ability to adapt, to become invisible, to scratch out an existence in the rubble-strewn alleys and the bombed-out buildings.

Most survived because of the kindness of strangers risking their lives to spare the life of a desperate child.

In a frantic attempt to save their children, some Jewish parents made the agonizing decision to leave their little ones in non-Jewish homes and institutions, separating their youngsters from everything they held dear: their families, friends and way of life.

Mine did not. We stayed together.

Many in desperation depended on strangers to help create false identities for their children – helping them learn new names and to memorize dates and places to support their false stories.

To blend in, many were baptized as Christians – or had false baptismal certificates made. However, any inconsistency could arouse suspicion. One slip could mean death – not only for the child, but also for their protectors.

From an early age, such children learned they had to contribute to everyone's safety by leaving their past behind and remaining silent.

For many, giving up their true identity

created an emotional void which lasted a lifetime.

Many of the youngest hidden children never knew they were Jewish.

Others learned years later.

But I knew who I was – *and what I was.*

I was the grandson of Rabbi Joseph Lewin and the son of Herman Lewin.

Chapter Four

As a young man, my father had worked for the railroad. However, one day he had an accident that badly injured his right leg, leaving him with a very noticeable limp for the rest of his life since his right leg was two inches shorter and much weaker than his left.

His hometown was little Schloppe in eastern Germany, in what today is western Poland. My father went to work for his father, my grandfather, the local rabbi, who also owned a clothing store that specialized in the finest furs and expensive attire.

Our town's little synagogue was a meeting room in the back of the store. Perhaps only 15 Jews lived in Schloppe. They did not flaunt their faith. Although we were Orthodox and strict, we dared not wear the skull caps or prayer shawls that would make us stand out.

Jews in Schloppe were held in some suspicion by the non-Jews, but my grandfather was a jovial, outgoing man who managed to cross over into non-Jewish society.

He was never completely accepted, but had good friends who were influential Gentiles. He got along with officials and local business owners. Looking back, I realize that he was greatly admired within the Schloppe community for his generosity. The non-Jews believed that he was wealthy, although he was not. But he gave back to the community.

It was his wife, my grim Grandmother Emma, who was his watchdog, making sure he didn't give away the store. Grandma Emma was the no-nonsense businesswoman – the one who made certain that a profit was made.

After the railway accident, my father had no choice but to work in the clothing store. There, he took after my grandmother – and became a salesman. His brother, my gentle Uncle Max, also worked in the store. He was more like my grandfather, though. He had a heart as big as a house.

We had the appearance of being secular Jews, yet as Orthodox, we observed many Jewish traditions, kept a kosher kitchen and avoided socializing too much outside the local Jewish community. Christians were held in suspicion. They were a bad influence. We could not count on them as true friends.

Our good friends, the Gotthilfs, had a successful business, too, and several children, so around 1934, they hired a pretty young Catholic girl named Hilda as their children's nanny. She did a good job.

She also caught the eye of my father.

That she was Catholic did not seem to bother him. After a long courtship that was opposed by both families, she and he were wed. It was not considered to be an ideal marriage since he was a Jew and she was a Christian.

She did not convert to Judaism. Religion was not a driving force in either of their lives. My father had rejected his traditional role as the rabbi's son and had no interest in becoming a member of the clergy.

Whatever my parents knew of their faith was cultural – rituals, ceremonies and traditions. Neither gave any thought to the idea that they could seek a personal relationship with the Creator of the Universe or receive His help.

Shortly after they were married, a great darkness began gathering over Europe. A terrible madness was unleashed from the very gates of hell. A twisted madman named Adolf Hitler rose to power in Germany, promising to return the nation to its pre-World War I glories.

When elected legislators got in his way, he burned down the Reichstag, Germany's Congress, and declared himself *Führer* – supreme leader.

His hypnotic, mesmerizing speeches stirred the German people, convincing them they were destined to rule the world. He told them that they were the master race, "Aryans" destined to dominate and subjugate the other inferior people of the planet. However, he declared, they needed to purge from their midst the evil parasites who diluted the power of the pure Germanic race – "sub-humans" such as gypsies and blacks and certainly Jews.

Politically, it was masterful. The German people were seduced into a national crusade against a common, vulnerable enemy. Even children could help – and feel patriotic. Persecuting Jews had political as well as material rewards: gangs of Nazis would drag elderly Jews out of their homes and humiliate the old, defenseless victims on the sidewalk while the rest of the gang rampaged through the house, looting it of valuables gathered over a lifetime. The police did nothing since everyone believed that the Jews were vastly wealthy and any valuables they had were ill-gotten.

Hitler's definition of "Jew" grew broad. Many people were branded as Jews although they did not consider themselves Jewish. If their grandparents' names were listed on synagogue rolls, they suddenly found themselves forced to wear a yellow Star of David on their clothes – branding them as an enemy of the state and a target of constant violence.

Hitler's Nuremberg Laws in 1935 stripped anyone defined as a Jew of all civil rights and German citizenship. Jews were separated legally, socially and politically – defined as an inferior race of "sub-humans" under the "Law for the Protection of German Blood and Honor."

Marriages or sexual relations between Jews and Germans were forbidden. Hitler convinced the German people that Jews had caused Germany's humiliating World War I defeat at the hands of the French, British and Americans.

From Holocaust to Hallelujah

Suddenly it was against the law to do business with Jews. Customers no longer filled my grandfather's store. In order to make a living, my mother and father had to go on the road and visit established customers who met with them privately behind closed doors.

It was a hard time for my mother. She was a frail-looking, 5-foot-2, 98-pound girl who had to follow behind my father, carrying heavy suitcases full of fur coats and suits and high-quality shirts and underthings. My father was a cruel man – he claimed that he could not carry the suitcases because of his leg injury.

So, she did what she had to do and soon became the darling of all the customers. Because of her good spirits and the fine quality of their wares, my parents managed to make a good living despite the new laws.

But in 1935, a complication arose. My mother was pregnant. She came home to Schloppe and gave birth to me, Dieter Daniel Lewin, on March 24, 1936.

That same year, Berlin hosted the Olympics. Hitler viewed this as a perfect opportunity to promote Nazism to the world. Monumental Olympic stadiums and arenas were constructed as Nazi showpieces. But in the land of "Aryan superiority," it was Jesse Owens, the African-American track star, who was the undisputed hero of the games.

It had been questioned whether the Nazis would really accept the terms of the Olympic Charter of participation unrestricted by class, creed or race. The Nazis guaranteed that they would allow German Jews to participate. Two Germans with some Jewish ancestry were invited to be on the German Olympic team, but the great German Jewish athlete, Gretel Bergmann, one of the world's most accomplished high jumpers, was not.

It was into this madness, this legal nightmare that I was born – not Jewish according to traditional Jewish religious law, which says a Jew is any person born of a Jewish mother – or anyone who converts to Judaism. Under either definition, I was not Jewish.

Yes, my father was a Jew by blood, but not my mother. To my own grandfather, the rabbi, I was a Gentile baby who as a teen would have to declare if I wanted to become truly Jewish.

However, the Nazis saw it differently. They considered Aryans the "master race" and natural leaders. They considered Jews to be "sub-human" and insidious enemies of the state. Even half-Jews were singled out to be eliminated.

Hitler assigned one of his closest henchmen, Heinrich Himmler, commander of the feared SS or *Schutzstaffel* stormtroopers to

From Holocaust to Hallelujah

enforce Hitler's every evil whim. The assignment to eradicate all Jewish life from German-occupied territory was given to Himmler. He placed Reinhard Heydrich directly in charge of the "Jewish question," utilizing the SS within Germany and the Nazi Gestapo police in the many territories that Germany conquered between 1939 and 1945. Heydrich assigned SS major Adolf Eichmann to the task. Before the war, Eichmann had visited Palestine and studied the Jewish religion and the Hebrew language.

His report to the leaders of the SS concerning his travels in the Holy Land convinced them that Eichmann was an expert on the subject. Eichmann became the head of the "Jewish desk" in Berlin, which gave him extraordinary – nearly absolute – power over the fate of the Jewish people in Germany and in all the conquered lands.

An initial idea apparently was to send all the Jews to Africa – perhaps to the German colonies of Uganda or Mauritius. Eichmann and Heydrich decided to gather as many Jews as possible into the Jewish ghettos that already existed all across Europe – and had since medieval times. All known Jews were forced to move out of their homes and congregate in these walled-off sections of the big cities.

These ghettos became staging areas for the deportation campaign. However, suffering from manpower shortages, the Nazis recognized that they were squandering a source of manual labor for the most degrading and undesirable work that nobody else wanted to do. So they allowed large German industries to "rent" these gathered-up Jews from the ghettos – paying them nothing, but getting their labor for large fees paid to the Gestapo.

Historians debate when it was that the Nazis decided not to deport the Jews, but to kill them. The term "Final Solution" was first used publicly in January 1942 when top Nazis met in Wannsee, a Berlin suburb. There, Heydrich read aloud what Eichmann had written was the "Final Solution of the Jewish Problem" – systematic extermination.

During that meeting, Russian Jews already were being regularly murdered by SS Einsatzgruppen squads, which followed close behind the Nazi advance into Soviet territories.

In each captured town, they rounded up the local rabbi and Jewish leaders, demanded a roster of all local Jews, then rousted everybody on the list. Men, women, children and the elderly were marched to secluded areas and ordered to dig long pits, remove all clothing, stack it in neat piles and wait in small groups to be taken down into the trench. There would be a burst of gunfire, then another group was marched in. One witness testified at the Nuremburg trials after the war:

"The pit was already two-thirds full. I estimated that it held a thousand people. I looked for the man who did the shooting. He was an SS man who sat at the edge of the narrow end of the pit, his feet dangling into it. He had a Thompson machine gun on his knees and was smoking a cigarette. The people – they were completely naked – went down some steps ... to the place where the SS man directed them. They lay down in front of the dead and wounded. Some caressed the living and spoke to them in a low voice. Then I heard a series of shots."

An estimated 33,000 were marched out of Kiev, the capital of the Ukraine, and gunned down in the Babi Yar ravine – the largest known massacre. However, Heydrich and Eichmann felt that the extermination was going too slowly. They searched for quicker ways that did not waste bullets.

Hitler suggested poison gas. As a soldier in World War I, he had been caught in a gas attack and still remembered the bitter, choking fear that had gripped him. In 1939 he had already been using gas to eliminate "imperfect

Aryans," Germans who were mentally ill or physically deformed. German doctors were ordered to give such newborns lethal injections, but told to experiment with gas on the adults.

Several German chemical companies competed for the lucrative contract to produce the most effective formula. Zyklon B was chosen – a powerful hydrogen cyanide manufactured by a company that specialized in pesticides for rats, cockroaches and lice.

Concentration camps were set up along the railroad lines. The ghettos were systematically emptied, the inhabitants told that they were being shipped out to work in "the east." Trains often arrived at the camps carrying tens of thousands Jews who had traveled for days without food, water or sanitation – often with people herded so tightly into cattle cars that there was only room to stand. Those who had died en route remained standing – wedged in between the living.

At the train platforms, loudspeakers blared, ordering the captives to get off the train, disrobe for showers, and prepare to work. Life now would be good, the officers shouted. The Jews would be given something constructive to do with their lives. Adults would work, children would go to school.

In shock, the new arrivals would often

refuse to move. German guards would open fire. Some Jews would try to run while others huddled on the train. The guards were trained to shout, "We know you want to die, but nothing will save you; you will have to go to work."

The terrified people were tricked into thinking that there really was work, not death, awaiting at their new home. The Nazis skillfully used hope and terror to keep the victims under control.

Inside the concentration camps, men, children and women were marched past a doctor who would raise his thumb left or right. The handicapped, injured, elderly, sick and most children under the age of 12 went left into the gas chambers. They were even given bars of soap and told to get clean for their new tasks.

Those who looked like they could do productive work were sent to the right and into the concentration camp's barracks. Of course no one knew what fate awaited them.

For those who marched left, the gas chambers' doors were bolted shut and the "shower rooms" were filled with gas. Screams could be heard by those marching right – who were given no time to grieve, but instead were driven like cattle into barracks with as many as 1,000 men, women and teens stuffed into long rooms built with only enough three- and four-tier bunks to accommodate 500.

Sanitary conditions were indescribable. Often only one bathroom, which typically was out of order, served large barracks. One survivor testified at Eichmann's trial after the war:

"From time to time we would get what they called 'soup.' Then they almost cut off the food supply altogether. Dead people lay outside on the paths of the camp. Women fought in the gutter for scraps of food garbage. At roll call we had to stand about for hours and hours in snow or rain, in heat or cold. The standing alone exhausted us entirely."

At another postwar trial for the officials at the Belsen concentration camp, a survivor testified: "If anyone was late for roll call, the whole camp had to stand on parade for many hours and he, the culprit, was beaten so badly that he sometimes died of it. We had 2,200 patients in the hospital and, in addition, 15,000 sick women in camp, but for a whole week we received only 300 aspirin tablets."

Within their first few days, thousands died of hunger, starvation and disease. Some threw themselves against the electrified fences – dying instantly. Still others died during cruelty that is almost unimaginable – such as "rabbit runs" in which prisoners were told to sprint across an enclosed courtyard. Guards used them for target practice, occasionally rewarding the last survivor by releasing him or her back to the barracks. At the Eichmann trial, one such survivor told of a contest among the Janowska guards:

"They would shoot out at the people marching back and forth loaded with stones, aiming at the tip of a nose or a finger. The injured people were 'no good' any more and they would finish them off with a shot."

Typhus, cholera, typhoid and encephalitis spread throughout the camps, but the sick pretended they were still healthy enough to work since sickness meant death. Even escape meant death, for if anyone escaped, all the other prisoners in that group were immediately shot.

The only defiance possible was simply to live. Prisoners fought to stay human and not descend to the level of animals. Many began to live an inner life, one that the guards and the camp could not reach or destroy. For many it was their faith.

Their trust in the Creator had been their mainstay on the outside. Now it became their inner treasure.

Others lost their faith – convinced that there could be no God who would allow such inhumanity.

For others, the key to retaining their sanity was work – such as doctors and nurses who tried to help the sick as best as possible. Scholars and journalists watched and memorized what they saw. In at least one case, a photographer made a makeshift camera and tried to record the unspeakable.

Viktor Frankl, a psychiatrist, wrote in his book, *Man's Search for Meaning,* of his efforts to help his fellow prisoners:

"The thought of suicide was entertained by nearly everyone, born of the hopelessness of the situation, the constant closeness of death.

"I told my comrades that human life, under any circumstances, never ceases to have a meaning. They must not lose hope but should keep up their courage in the certainty that the hopelessness of our struggle did not detract from its dignity and meaning.

"I said that someone looks down on each of us in difficult hours – a friend, a wife, somebody alive or dead or a Heavenly Father – and He would not expect us to disappoint Him. He would hope to find us suffering proudly."

Thousands of bodies were placed in huge furnaces. The smell of death rose with the smoke and ashes, which pumped out of the chimneys and could be seen and smelled for miles around.

More than six millions Jews walked into the death camps.

Few walked out.

Chapter Five

Before all the deportations started, back when I was only six months old, my parents had gone back on the road, selling high-quality clothing. Finances had gotten tight with the new laws prohibiting Jews from doing business. We had to make a living, however – and my parents began calling privately on longtime customers, who were generally glad to see them.

Back in Schloppe, my Uncle Max took over my care. It is said that he was a real mother

From Holocaust to Hallelujah

hen. He was in his 20s and was delighted with me. He helped me take my first steps and heard my first words. He would take me on daily walks with his chest puffed out in pride. No child ever had a more devoted uncle than I did.

But I received so much love from everyone. The Almighty provided me with a foundation of love and care that most children have never experienced.

I was only two years old on November 9-10, 1938 when our lives were changed forever on "Kristallnacht," the "Night of Broken Glass."

Over two terrible nights, 8,000 Jewish-owned businesses throughout Germany were destroyed in mob riots led by Hitler's street-thug paramilitary militia, the brown-shirts, assisted by SS stormtroopers and the young criminals-in-training who were Hitler Youth.

My grandparents' store was not hit. But overnight, they were even more distrusted and resented than ever before. This was hard for them to understand as they were extremely loyal to Germany. Our family, although Orthodox, had never flaunted our Jewishness had been largely assimilated into Schloppe society.

However, we were relatively prosperous. And that made us targets of resentment.

Throughout Germany, many Jews had small shops as well as large factories. They served prominently in the German armed forces and contributed to German science, business and culture. German Jews included the 1905 Nobel Prize winner for chemistry Adolf von Baeyer, 1915 Nobel Prize winner for chemistry Fritz Haberze, the 1925 Nobel Prize winner for physics James Franck and the 1921 Nobel Prize winner for physics, Albert Einstein.

But once the Nazis seized power, Jews were progressively demonized and by 1938 had been almost completely excluded from German social and political life. Many sought asylum abroad – leaving for America. However, my grandparents and parents saw no reason to flee the land of their ancestors. Hitler was just one more politician.

Their attitude was "this, too, shall pass." My father adamantly declared he was a loyal German. He was not about to leave.

Those who did flee became pariahs on the international scene. Nobody wanted Germany's refugee Jews. German law prohibited them from taking any savings or valuables with them, so they arrived penniless – in many people's eyes a cursed people who collectively bore the guilt and shame for Jesus' crucifixion.

From Holocaust to Hallelujah

Author Chaim Weizmann wrote, "The world seemed to be divided into two parts – those places where the Jews could not live and those where they could not enter." Even America turned away boats filled with desperate refugees, such as the *SS Saint Louis*.

Historian Eric Johnson writes that Germany "entered a new radical phase" in the campaign to discredit all Jews.

Zionists in Palestine had warned in February 1938 that they had heard from "a very reliable private source – one which can be traced back to the highest echelons of the SS leadership," that there was "an intention to carry out a genuine and dramatic pogrom in Germany on a large scale in the near future."

A pogrom is a campaign against Jews – such as you might remember from the musical *The Fiddler on the Roof* in which government officials not only sanctioned, but were required to persecute their local Jewish population, often with the reward of looting or confiscating Jewish possessions.

Kristallnacht came about after about 17,000 Polish Jews living in Germany, many for more than 10 years, were arrested and taken to the Polish-German border and forced to leave Germany – not far from where my family lived.

The Polish border guards sent them back over into Germany. A stalemate continued for days in the pouring rain with Jews marching without food or shelter between borders until the Polish government admitted them to a concentration camp.

The conditions of the camp was "were so bad that some actually tried to escape back into Germany and were shot" reported a British relief worker sent to help the expellees.

Two of these Polish Jews had a son named Henry Grynszpan, who was living in Paris. The seventeen-year-old was frantic with concern for his parents and felt that he needed to "do" something to publicize to the world what was happening.

The boy got a gun, walked to the German embassy in Paris and shot the first man he saw, an embassy official named Ernst Von Rath. Von Rath died two days later on November 9.

Word of Von Rath's "assassination" reached Hitler during his "Old Fighters" dinner with several key members of the Nazi party. Hitler left abruptly without giving his scheduled address.

Propaganda Minister Joseph Goebbels instead delivered a speech, announcing in typical Nazi double-talk that the Führer had decided that no protest demonstrations should be prepared or organized by the Nazi Party.

However – and here's how the Nazis invariably talked out of both sides of their mouth – should nationwide riots erupt "spontaneously," they were not to be hampered.

A top Nazi judge, Walter Buch, later wrote that Goebbels' message was clear – nationwide, local Nazi leaders were *expected* to organize vandalism and murder targeting the Jews.

Behind the scenes, some leading Nazi officials disagreed, fearing the diplomatic crisis it could provoke. Himmler even went so far as to write "I suppose that it is Goebbels's megalomania and stupidity which are responsible for starting this operation now, in a particularly difficult diplomatic situation."

At 1:20 a.m. on November 10, 1938, Reinhard Heydrich sent an urgent secret telegram to "All Headquarters and Stations of the State Police, All Districts and Sub-districts" containing instructions regarding the riots.

And then the nationwide "spontaneous" rioting began. Most of the vandals wore civilian clothes and were armed with sledgehammers and axes. Their orders were very specific – no measures endangering non-Jewish property. Synagogues too close to non-Jewish German property were smashed rather than burned, for example.

Jewish businesses or dwellings were to be destroyed but not looted. No rioting was authorized against foreigners, even if they were Jewish. All synagogue records were to be carefully preserved and given to Nazi officials. As many Jews as the local jails would hold were to be arrested – with a focus on wealthy, young, healthy males.

Overnight, Jewish homes and stores were ransacked throughout Germany and Austria, leaving the streets covered in smashed glass from the windows of the destroyed businesses the next morning – hence, the name "Crystal Night."

About 1,575 synagogues and cemeteries were desecrated and vandalized. More than 7,000 Jewish shops and 29 department stores were put out of business. More than 30,000 Jewish males were arrested and taken to concentration camps at Dachau, Buchenwald and Sachsenhausen.

As many as 300 Jews were killed and hundreds of suicides were reported in the following days as whatever hope that had remained disappeared completely.

Damage to synagogues, cemeteries and other sacred sites were described as "approaching the ghoulish" by the United States Consul in Leipzig, where tombstones were uprooted and graves violated.

Bonfires lit the sky, destroying prayer books, sacred scrolls and artwork. Eric Lucas recalls the destruction of the synagogue that a tiny Jewish community had constructed in a small village only twelve years earlier:

"It did not take long before the first heavy grey stones came tumbling down, and the children of the village amused themselves as they flung stones into the many colored windows.

"When the first rays of a cold and pale November sun penetrated the heavy dark clouds, the little synagogue was but a heap of stone, broken glass and smashed-up woodwork."

It cost 4 million marks alone to repair the windows nationwide. Most of Vienna's 94 synagogues and prayer-houses were vandalized or destroyed. Jews were subjected to public humiliation, including being forced to scrub the pavements while being tormented by fellow Austrians.

The violence was officially called to a stop by Goebbels on November 11, but still continued.

Top Nazi official Hermann Göring met with other members of the Nazi leadership on November 12 to plan the next steps after the rioting, setting the stage for formal government action. In a transcript of the meeting, Göring is quoted as saying,

"I have received a letter written on the Führer's orders requesting that the Jewish question be now, once and for all, coordinated and solved one way or another. I should not want to leave any doubt, gentlemen, as to the aim of today's meeting.

"We have not come together merely to talk again, but to make decisions, and I implore competent agencies to take all measures for the elimination of the Jew from the German economy, and to submit them to me."

German Jews were ordered to pay the "Judenvermögensabgabe," a fine of 1 billion reichsmarks (about $5.5 billion) for von Rath's assassination in Paris.

"Since few Jewish businesses could pay, their property was confiscated – resulting in about 20 percent of Jewish-owned property being seized by the Nazis.

In the next ten months, more than 115,000 Jews emigrated from the Reich. The majority went to other European countries, the U.S. and British Palestine, and at least 14,000 made it to Shanghai, China.

Several nations condemned the acts. *The Times of London* commented: "No foreign propagandist bent upon blackening Germany before the world could outdo the tale of burnings and beatings, of blackguardly assaults on defenseless and innocent people, which disgraced that country yesterday."

The Nazis suffered almost no international repercussions. They interpreted the lack of global reaction that the world would tolerate persecution on a mass scale.
The average German citizen's reaction was similar. German witness Dr. Arthur Flehinger recalled seeing "people crying while watching from behind their curtains."
Some even went as far as to help Jews on Kristallnacht, but the vast majority merely sat inside watching in horror, feeling helpless to do anything.
In an article released for publication on the evening of November 11, Goebbels said the events of Kristallnacht occurred because of the "healthy instincts" of the German people not "to be provoked in the future by parasites of the Jewish race."

Kristallnacht changed the nature of official persecution of the Jews from economic, political and social to physical – such as beatings, murder and incarceration.
Historian Max Rein wrote, "Kristallnacht came ... and everything was changed."
Germany's Jews finally got the message.
But where were we to go?

Chapter Six

The day after my grandparents were arrested, believing that we could be safe in Berlin instead of trying to flee to Switzerland or France, my father drove to the capital.

He thought we could get lost in a big city.

However, his unorthodox plan fell apart almost immediately. We could not get an apartment until we registered with the police. Anyone renting to a Jew found without a valid registration would be arrested and taken to a concentration camp.

So, my father had to confess to being a Jew

– and submit to wearing the yellow star. However, my mother was not required to do so. And in Berlin, only children older than 13 wore the stars.

So, I was exempt.

However, we found out quickly that life in Berlin was not as good as my father had expected.

There was no way for a Jew wearing the star to be inconspicuous. Jews were prohibited from any professional job, from receiving medical care, attending school or having contact with Gentiles.

However, my father's plan actually worked. In 1933, the Jewish population of Berlin had been about 160,000. Berlin's Jewish community was the largest in Germany, comprising more than 32 percent of all Jews in the country. As Nazi persecution grew worse, many fled from Berlin. The city's Jewish population fell to about 80,000.

Without a doubt, the Jews of Berlin faced persecution and discrimination. Jewish civil servants and professionals were fired or barred from practicing. Books written by Jews were publicly burned in front of the opera house.

However, the first deportations of Jews from Berlin did not start for several years.

It was not until October 1941 that assembly areas were established at synagogues on

Levetzow Street and Heidereuter Alley, at the Jewish cemetery on Grosse Hamburger Street and on Rosen Street. About 1,000 or so Jews were assembled at a time, taken to the freight yards at Grunewald, then loaded onto boxcars like cattle.

But when we arrived in 1938, Berlin was relatively safe for Jews – compared to the rest of Germany and the territories it was conquering.

How could my father have known that? Four years later, only about 10,000 of Berlin's Jews had been deported, mostly to work camps. When the war began to go badly for the Nazis, deportation was increased dramatically. In fact, in the final days of the war, even Jews the Nazis had forced to oversee the deportations, such as the Reich Association of Jews in Germany, were arrested and murdered.

All Jewish organizations were disbanded. Constantly anyone wearing the yellow star on the street was subject to surprise roundups – and disappeared.

Hundreds of Jews committed suicide rather than submit to the deportations. Even so, there was a remnant that remained in Berlin, mostly those who had gone into hiding – posing as non-Jewish.

Then, there were those with a non-Jewish spouse. Although it was my father who was inspired to get us to Berlin, it was actually my mother's non-Jewishness that saved us.

Nevertheless, we experienced extreme prejudice. We not allowed to travel or change residence without the permission of the police. My parents were assigned menial jobs and had to work from 7 a.m. to 6 p.m.

My father worked in the rail yards in Berlin. My mother was given a job in a large department store. They were paid substandard wages – but that was allowed since they were a Jew and the wife of a Jew.

My mother had to work if we were to pay the rent and eat. That presented a serious problem since I was only a toddler. What was she to do with me?

We had no family in Berlin. We made few friends. No non-Jew dared have anything to do with us socially.

We did not have money to pay for food, much less a nanny. No one would work for a Jew anyway. We were considered to be less than human.

Often she and I broke the law and rode on the streetcars sitting in the front where Jews weren't allowed – and avoided any trouble since we did not look Jewish and were not standing in the back with the Jews. Even the chimpanzees and gorillas in the Berlin Zoo were considered better than Jews.

The Nazis were much like the Ku Klux Klan during the 1920-50s in America. Some people joined the Klan because they hated blacks. Others joined because they thought they had to, maybe to keep their job or to avoid being targeted themselves – even though they would never hurt a black person if they had to. I have spent years living in America's beautiful South and I have seen it myself: hate tolerated by an intimidated or indifferent majority.

In Germany, there were a very small few who said, "I'm not joining that." But, if you wanted a job, you had to join the Party.

As a result, there were hard-core Nazis, and then there were Nazi Party members who were not true believers but did nothing to stop the madness.

There were some who were real Nazis, who were no good and wanted to kill all the Jews. Then there were others who could care less, who just went along because their jobs and their positions depended on it. If you owned a factory and you wanted to sell to the German government, you'd better join the Nazi party, because that was who was going to get the contracts.

And so, after the war was over, the real

Nazis shut up because they knew it was dangerous to be found out by the Russians or the Americans – or, later, the Israelis.

Chapter Seven

As a two-year-old approaching my third birthday, I could not stay alone in our apartment while my parents worked.

My mother learned that other children of Jews being allowed to work spent their days at the city dump. No Jewish child was allowed in German public schools – and all Jewish private academies had been forcibly closed.

I have only vague memories of meeting a couple of teenage girls and walking with them and my parents to what seemed to be a wonderland – a vast municipal dump overflowing with piles and heaps of junk, trash and garbage on every side.

The smell was astonishing for a little boy – a sickening-sweet mixture of burning paper, rotting garbage and stagnant water, but there was so much to do! I thought it was a paradise – wrecked cars, broken toilets, discarded remains of buildings ... and piles and piles of wonderful cast-offs to dig through, build castles in and play hide-and-seek in.

I vaguely remember how quite a number of Jewish children, most older than me, hesitantly came out of hiding when they saw my father's yellow star. My parents told me to go with them, stay out of sight and to obey the older girls.

It was exciting. The older kids kept a lookout for the police and for gangs of Hitler Youth – who enjoyed beating up Jewish kids. We were not allowed to fight back. But we could hide. Or run.

We hid whenever we heard that the police were coming – either on bicycle or in cars on their daily rounds. That was a great game, too, particularly when I was too little to know how serious it was. We would hide and be very, very still.

One of my most vivid memories is of playing in the old, wrecked cars – pretending to be a fighter pilot or a bus driver or a race-car driver, making motor noises. It was the only car I got to ride in for years.

Jews traveled very little as it became increasingly unsafe. Jews were frequently attacked by Nazi thugs who "guarded" the train stations.

Since Mother and I didn't look Jewish, and she wasn't required to wear the star, we carefully concealed our true identities the one time that we traveled to visit her parents.

My mother's family had not formally disowned her for marrying a Jew, but there was very little communication. Finally, she contacted them and we went to visit.

I remember it as a long, miserable journey. I had to sit quietly, without running around or talking to anyone or playing with any children my age.

I was sternly warned not to reveal we were Jewish to anyone and not to talk to strangers. Whenever I saw Nazi thugs in the distance, I was to cross to the other side of the road.

I feared those brown-shirts and Hitler Youth. They looked menacing and cruel to me, even though I couldn't truly understand the deadly threat they represented.

When we arrived in Langenbielau, a small town in northeastern Germany, we were warmly greeted by all. It was the first time that I had met all of the family on my mother's side.

My cousin Rosel was the same age as me, so we had a great time together. It was the genesis of many things for me. It was the first time I tasted milk. It was the first time I could go out in the countryside and play with other children.

We went wild strawberry picking in the nearby mountains and then got to eat some of them soaked in milk.

I saw cows, goats and chickens. We picked cherries. All in all, it was the best time of my life. Jewish persecution hadn't arrived there yet, so they were not at risk of being seen with us.

We had a tearful goodbye and took the long trip back to Berlin. When we arrived, it was just after one of the earliest Allied bombings. Our apartment house had taken a direct hit and was leveled. Once again, we had only what we possessed in our bags. My father hadn't been home – he'd stayed too late at a friend's house and spent the night rather than risk being caught out after curfew.

We lived on the street for several days before he found us another place to live.

On another occasion, my mother and I actually traveled to visit my father's parents at the concentration camp. My father did not dare come with us. I remember a large, dismal place surrounded by high fences and barbed wire, filled with endless rows of barracks. Only a few bare trees stood back from the cleared areas around the fences, adding a look of terrible sadness to the desolation. As a small child, I remember being frightened as a guard examined our papers.

He yelled at my mother, berating her for wanting to visit Jews. After she quietly handed over a small bribe, he raised the barrier and directed us to another guard. He, too, taunted her before shamelessly pocketing another small bribe.

After a long wait, we were allowed to enter a room where my grandparents were sitting nervously. We thought it was their apartment – but, in fact, it was where prisoners met with the International Red Cross. They had nice clothes and blankets – which they had been given only for the day. They had to pretend this was their quarters.

Very subdued and much thinner than when we had last seen them as they were forced onto the truck, they hugged me awkwardly.

We did not know that the guards were listening in – and that my grandparents had been told that if they told us the truth about the concentration camp, my mother and I would not be allowed to leave. During the long, miserable journey home, Mother did not speak much between her sobs and long sighs.

In the next weeks and months, we began to hear horrible stories – of Jews in the concentration camps being shot when they got too sick or weak to work, of elderly Jews stripped naked in the winter cold, doused with icy water and forced to stand at attention and freeze to death. Of defiant young Jews being beaten to death with nightsticks in front of everybody.

Although those stories were terrifying enough, we did not hear the truth – of the gas chambers that had quietly begun murdering 1,000 at a time nor of the crematoriums burning tens of thousands of bodies.

That was the last time I saw my grandparents. They died in the camp, apparently gassed to death when they became too weak to work.

We received no notice.

I have no idea where they are buried – or if they were cremated. I have heard stories of how some Jews were boiled for their body fat, which was made into bars of soap, which were given to the other prisoners as a sick Nazi joke.

In one museum, there is a lampshade made

of human skin – the hideous handiwork of Nazi ghouls experimenting with ways to use the bodies.

I have learned not to think about such things – lest I become bitter and resentful. Instead, I choose to remember my grandfather as the big, jovial, generous rabbi who made a living selling high-quality clothing. As I close my eyes, I can still see my loving but stern grandmother. She loved her little grandson.

They protected me there at the concentration camp by not saying a word about the nightmare in which they were living.

When Germany broke its pact with the Soviets and invaded Russia, we did not listen on the radio to Hitler's impassioned speeches as he denounced the "Jew Bolsheviks" and promised their complete annihilation.

When the Führer came on, my father would turn off the radio. He could not bear to listen to the madman. He had read Hitler's book, *Mein Kampf,* but had not taken seriously his anti-Jewish rantings. Now my father began to see just how badly he had misjudged the book and its mad author.

Discrimination against Jews was now rampant in every branch of the armed services and Jewish servicemen were subjected to every kind of humiliation and physical punishment.

He had heard of the terrible treatment Jews were receiving in German-occupied territories, but nobody knew the full story.

We knew of the ghettos that Jews were being herded into by the tens of thousands. We heard of the atrocities committed in Austria and Poland.

But extermination camps and mass executions were not yet public knowledge. We heard of how Jewish communities were being evacuated and of how those who were deported just disappeared to some unknown destination.

We could not fathom what the Nazi-controlled press described as the "final solution" to the "Jewish question."

Hitler Youth and Nazi thugs constantly paraded in the streets with their banners and flags, spouting Nazi propaganda and attacking Jewish-looking passers-by or anyone who looked Jewish – including innocent riders on the streetcars.

During the gang beatings, other passengers watched or looked away.

My "Aryan" appearance saved me. But as a small child, it left deep impressions as I saw fellow Jews being slapped around and kicked off streetcars. My mother was terrified. She felt like a tiny mouse trying to avoid the attention of the cat.

From Holocaust to Hallelujah

By 1941, hundreds of thousands of German Jews worked in forced labor camps. Many 16- to 48-year-old Jewish men – like my father – were virtual slave laborers, forced to do menial work – regardless of their training or abilities.

But instead of being dragged away, my father was allowed to stay with us and work in a Berlin factory. Why? I was too small to question things.

I know now that it was because the Jews in Berlin were among the last to be deported.

And, there was his marriage to my mother.

As the street round-ups of Jews increased, he was actually arrested twice – and headed for a concentration camp. Both times, my mother rushed to the police station and somehow got him released.

I was taken along to the police station, but was too small to know all that was going on. I remember sitting in cruel Nazi officials' offices and being concerned as my mother cried and pleaded on my father's behalf.

Incredibly, both times, they let him go.

That was unheard of.

But at least twice, my mother saved my father from certain death.

Chapter Eight

When I turned five, I was not allowed to enroll in kindergarten since no Jewish children were permitted in school.

Both of my parents worked 11 hours a day for tiny wages – and had to walk home many times when they were denied a ride on the street cars.

I spent long hours in the city dump. A terrible danger I faced was from gangs of Nazi boys who stalked the streets and beat up Jewish children. My non-Jewish appearance saved me many times. I can only remember being beaten twice – since I was a very fast runner and quite good at hiding.

Neither beating stands out in my memory – only as something very bad that happened to me when I didn't manage to run fast enough.

Neither experience was life-threatening, just humiliating and intimidating.

Both times, my tormentors pulled down my pants and hooted in derision when they saw I was circumcised – the mark of the covenant that the Lord had made with Abraham.

I became proud of how fast I could run. Jews were forbidden to fight back. But I could run. And if the Hitler Youth couldn't catch me, they couldn't hurt me.

My parents would drop me off at the dump around 5:30 a.m., then would not return until after dark – when I would meet my mother at a designated spot around 7 p.m.

Most of the time, I just played with the other children my age at the dump – and hid when police or Hitler Youth were spotted. I do not remember anybody's names. Four- and five-year-olds do not demand papers or family histories. We were just children playing together, trying not to think about the terrible nightmare all around us. It was actually best that we knew nothing about one another.

Frequently one of my playmates would just disappear – a sure sign that his family had been arrested and deported to a camp. But since we didn't know their names or where they lived, we did not attempt to find them.

They were just gone.

Sometimes in the dump, we found wonderful things, such as a toy airplane or a remnant of a cake. We each turned into treasure hunters – scrambling over the piles and piles of refuse, keeping clear of the dump's adult workers – trying to be invisible.

It seemed we were always hungry and cold.

There really weren't that many of us – certainly no more than 15 at a time – and the dump was vast.

Why didn't the police figure out that a bunch of Jewish children were hiding out at the dump?

I don't know.

Chapter Nine

The war came to Berlin in earnest in 1943 when the British and American air forces began a combined air assault on the city. With the Americans bombing by day and the British by night, the Allies delivered constant death and destruction to the city.

This was before "smart bombs" that could pinpoint key targets. As a result, neighborhoods in the poorer parts of town next to factories or train stations were devastated.

My father would turn on the radio

whenever we heard air-raid sirens. The announcer would report that airplanes had been sighted over Rotterdam or Hamburg or wherever. That gave us plenty of time to head for the shelters.

We sat in darkness. Lighting was kept to a minimum. Later when power stations and overhead wires were hit by Allied bombs, it was cut off completely. Windows and doors were kept covered so no light would escape, but this also kept the weak outside light from coming in.

Streetcars began traveling without lighting or heat. Riders huddled in their rags, cursing under their frozen breath.

By the time my mother got off work and came to get me at the dump, then finally reached the streetcar stop, Berlin was in total darkness and the streets were practically deserted. The streetcar would come, darkened and in silence.

I remember being disappointed when the merry ring of the conductor's bell ceased.

Jews with work permits were allowed to ride the street cars, but not to sit, not even when the streetcar was empty.

We were supposed to stand crowded together in an open area at the back of the car, fully exposed to the cold and blowing winds.

From Holocaust to Hallelujah

No Jew was exempt, not women, not the elderly, not the sick.

My family's long walk from the streetcar to our apartment through the chilly, dark streets was made in silence. With our hands shaking from the cold, we would open the door and enter our freezing rooms. We talked very little. There was so little to say and my parents were exhausted from the long days of tedious work.

I remember a serious water shortage when it became impossible to take showers. Each family in our building would take turns. A small wash basin was filled with water and served as a mini-bathtub.

There were constant food shortages and ration books were required. This meant you could only get so many grams of bread, so many eggs per week, and so on. It also meant spending many hours lining up outside bakeries and grocery stores. Our diet was reduced to the most basic food items: black bread, beans, corn, dry peas and potatoes.

Food became a serious worry for everyone, especially Jews. Our ration cards were stamped with big J's identifying us as Jews and entitling us to lesser quantities. Often the storekeeper would look at our card, throw it back and say, "There's no more food," then kick us out.

We only survived because there were some kind storekeepers who took the risk to help Jews and families of Jews, but they were very few.

My mother went through garbage cans on her way home from work. She usually salvaged potato peels.

Dinner was generally a watery soup with cooked vegetables, scavenged potato peels and hard, black bread. It was all my mother could provide. Little did we know that the most nutritious vitamins and minerals in a potato are found in the peels!

We ate in silence, trying not to complain. I went to sleep every night hungry, dreaming of some big meal I could remember at my Uncle Max's house or at a party hosted by my grandparents.

In the dump, we would play a game of "banquet" in which we pretended that a vast table had been set and we were eating goose and roast beef and cakes and puddings.

Steadily, the situation deteriorated as the war got worse for Germany. Jews were ordered to hand over all items of value, such as jewels, coins and foreign currency. Jewish presence in any business or professional activity was forbidden. My father was barred from trying to set up any kind of business.

Jews were only allowed to be outside

during certain hours of the day. Since Jews could only be out on the street at certain times, we couldn't go to the stores to look for leftover food. We couldn't travel long distances for fear of not being back home on time.

We were banned from all public places, except stores. We weren't allowed to go into restaurants or attend movies – even if we could have afforded it.

When people saw my father's yellow star, I remember how some looked away. Others lowered their eyes as they passed us. Still others looked straight at him with a mocking grin. Then there were some who looked offended – as if my father had no right to be there.

Those often would make comments about Jews being traitors and cowards, dirty, lice-ridden sub-humans who deserved the worst.

But far worse were the roving bands of hooligans who were actually encouraged to victimize Jews. Their vicious attacks were humiliating and could be deadly. I was never physically abused in the streetcar, the way I witnessed some older Jews being attacked.

The streetcar would be stopped by brown shirts or Hitler Youth who would demand, "Any Jews here?! Does anybody see any Jews here?"

If they did, they would be dragged out and beaten up, then left on the street. Ugly scenes played out more and more often, with indignant "patriots" insisting that a Jew be arrested for not wearing the star.

Some policemen still behaved with a degree of decency. They would just issue a warning and tell the "criminal" to disappear quickly. Such simple acts were so outstanding. But why didn't more people behave like human beings?

The word "deportation" quickly became part of our vocabulary. Officially, it meant moving all Jews to unknown areas in the east, where we would be resettled and allowed to live and work peacefully.

If we had only known the truth.

To millions of Jews, it meant being ordered without warning to pack a small bag and report to a specific point, like an abandoned factory or a stone quarry.

They were marched through the streets of towns and villages where Germans lined up along both sides, some watching sadly and even quietly crying. Others gloated with satisfaction with the revenge being taken against us Jews.

Most, however, were apathetic and looked away – pretending nothing was happening.

During these marches, many of the sick and elderly were shot or beaten to death on the road if they were unable to keep up. Traveling in packed cattle cars, they were locked up, with even the windows covered with barbed wire, to an unknown destination, an unknown fate. At the train station, there was confusion, shouting and yelling as one group after another was pushed up into cattle cars.

Railway stations were guarded by soldiers and declared out-of-bounds to the civilian population. But the railway workers were there and heard the cries and pleadings.

Some risked their own safety to smuggle cans of water into the cattle cars or to pick up little pieces of paper thrown out through the barbed wire-covered windows, with names and phone numbers of relatives to call. The workers delivered these sad messages and proved to be decent human beings.

I have tried to watch Holocaust movies such as *Sophie's Choice*, *The Hiding Place* and *Schindler's List*. It may be entertainment or enlightening or educational to some. But for me, it is a return to a terrible experience that my mind has tried to blot from my memory.

The saddest victims were the children.

Chapter Ten

In November 1944, twenty newly arrived Jewish children, were brought from Auschwitz to the concentration camp of Neuengamme, just outside Hamburg, Germany.

The youngsters, aged between 5 and 12 years old, came from all over Europe and were to be human guinea-pigs in a series of medical experiments conducted by Dr. Kurt Heissmeyer.

First he removed their lymph glands for analysis, then he injected living tuberculosis bacteria into their veins and directly into their lungs to determine if they had any natural immunities to tuberculosis. They were carefully observed, examined and photographed as the disease progressed. The condition of all the children deteriorated very rapidly and each became extremely ill.

On April 20, 1945, the day on which Adolf Hitler was celebrating his 56th birthday and just a few days before the war ended, Heissmeyer and SS Obersturmführer Arnold Strippel decided to kill the children in an effort to hide evidence of the experiments from the approaching Allied forces.

To conceal all traces, the SS transported the children to the former Bullenhuser Damm School, which had been used as a satellite camp since October 1944. They were taken to the basement and ordered to undress.

An SS officer later reported: "They sat down on the benches all around and were cheerful and happy that they had been for once allowed out of Neuengamme. The children were completely unsuspecting."

The children were told that they had to be vaccinated against typhoid fever before their return journey. Then they were injected with morphine. As each lost consciousness, they were hanged by the neck from hooks on the wall, but the first child to be strung up was so light – due to disease and malnutrition – that the rope wouldn't strangle him.

Untersturmführer Frahm had to use all of his own weight to tighten the noose. Then he hanged the others, two at a time, from different hooks. 'Just like pictures on the wall,' he would recall later. He added that none of the children cried.

At five o' clock in the morning on April 21, 1945, the Nazis had finished with their work and each had a cup of coffee.

One of the children was Jacqueline Morgenstern, born to Suzanne and Karl Morgenstern in 1932 in Paris, France. Here Jacqueline had led a happy life, she attended school and her father and uncle owned a beauty shop in central Paris.

The family's feelings of security collapsed, however, when in 1940, Germany invaded France. In 1944 Jacqueline and her parents were sent to Auschwitz. Jacqueline and her mother went to the women's work camp, where food rations were meager.

Suzanne gave Jacqueline most of her food, so she became malnourished and ill. When the Nazis found her too weak to work, they sent her to the gas chambers.

After her mother's death, Jacqueline was sent to a special children's barrack. The majority of the children spoke only Polish but one of the boys, Georges Andre Kohn, spoke French and they became close friends.

Kohn was 12 years old and the youngest son of Armand Kohn, a rich Jewish businessman in Paris.

In 1944 Georges, his 75-year-old grandmother, mother, father, older sisters Rose-Marie and Antoinette, and his 18-year-old brother Philippe were crowded into cattle cars with hundreds of Jews to be deported to the Buchenwald concentration camp.

Three days after the train began moving, Rose-Marie and Philippe broke the bars of the car's small window, jumped out and escaped.

Georges and the rest of the family was taken to Buchenwald.

Chapter Eleven

Where was God?

On April 6, 1944 the Nazis sent two vans to the French village of Izieu. Their mission was to raid a Catholic orphanage known as La Maison d'Izieu.

The sleepy village of Izieu lay overlooking the Rhone River between Lyon and Chambery in central France. Refugees from Herault were the first arrivals at the Children's home and their Jewish identity was kept secret by the staff. The children, aged between four and 17, felt safe and secure, supervised by seven nuns.

Often one of the young boys entertained his companions by making movies, paintings on transparent paper and scrolled past a lighted box.

However, on the morning of April 6, as they all settled down in the refectory to drink hot chocolate, Nazi vehicles pulled up in front of the home. The Gestapo, led by the "Butcher of Lyon" Klaus Barbie, entered the home and forcibly removed the 44 children, throwing them, crying and terrified, onto the trucks like sacks of potatoes.

As a witness later recalled: "I was on my way down the stairs when my sister shouted to me: it's the Germans, save yourself! I jumped out the window. I hid myself in a bush in the garden. I heard the cries of the children and I heard the shouts of the Nazis who were carrying them away."

Following the raid, the children were put on the first available train to the death camps in the East. Forty-two were gassed at Auschwitz. Two were put to death by firing squad.

Of the forty-four children, not a single one survived. Of the nuns there was one sole survivor, 27-year-old Lea Feldblum. When the children from Izieu arrived in Auschwitz on April 15, 1944, she led the column of children to the selection point. When she informed the guards that these children were from a Catholic home, she was roughly separated from them and sent to the prisoners' camp.

During Klaus Barbie's trial a witness testified: "I asked myself where were the children who arrived? In the camp there wasn't a single child to be seen. Then those who had been there for a while informed us of the reality. 'You see that chimney, the one smoke never stops coming out of. Smell that odor of burned flesh?'"

One of the children was eleven-year-old Liliane Gerenstein. She and her brother were sent to their deaths only a few days after she wrote this letter that was found in the empty orphanage:

"God? How good You are, how kind and if one had to count the number of goodnesses and kindnesses You have done, one would never finish.

"God? It is You who command. It is You who are justice, it is You who reward the good and punish the evil.

"God? It is thanks to You that I had a beautiful life before, that I was spoiled, that I had lovely things that others do not have.

"God? After that, I ask You one thing only: Make my parents come back, my poor parents protect them (even more than You protect me) so that I can see them again as soon as possible.

"Make them come back again. Ah! I had such a good mother and such a good father! I have such faith in You and I thank You in advance."

Another survivor, Kitty Saks, says that decades later, she still feels anger toward the Nazis.

"I'll never forget what they did," she recalls. "It was absolutely madness. It was a mad world that we came from. How would you like someone to come into your house and take over? I mean, it's unheard of to be evicted from your own home, to be thrown out of your own country because you're a Jew."

But that's exactly what happened to Kitty. When she was only 6, the Nazis took over Kitty's home in Austria. Looking for an escape, she and her parents fled to Belgium.

"It became extremely difficult for me to accept the fact that we were on the run and we had to leave," she remembers. "I couldn't understand. I just couldn't understand. We had to wear the yellow star to identify us as Jews. Then we could no longer go to see a physician. No Jew could go to the theater. No Jew could go to the park."

As life for Jews became more and more endangered, Kitty's parents went into hiding. Kitty was befriended by her gym teacher,

Fernan Herar, a devout Belgian Catholic.

"She saw me walking the streets one day and she said, 'Kitty, I think it's very dangerous for you to walk around displaying your star. I want to place you in a convent.'

Why would she want to do such a thing? In doing so, she was taking an enormous risk herself.

"She said, 'I'm my brother's keeper,'" recalls Kitty. She placed many – I'm not the only one. She placed many children in convents, orphanages, boarding schools with Christians, whoever wanted to take us in."

Kitty took refuge in a convent where she became a Christian.

"In this particular convent where I was finally placed, after many attempts to place me, it had to be, and I realized it had to be. I had to blend in. I was 9 years old going on 10. Mrs. Harrar said, 'Your name is no longer Kitty Friedenbach. It is now Rosette Nizolle.' She made me repeat this over and over: 'Rosette Nizolle, Rosette Nizolle.' 'You don't speak German. You only speak French. You're not Jewish. You're Catholic.' That day, I became a hidden child.

"To me, it was like being in a play where I made it up as I went along. It was not really lying. It was being in a play where I had to just do my part, change my part. I was baptized. First, I was given lessons in catechism by one of the nuns."

When she was alone at night in bed and lying there thinking, she prayed. Was she confused – unsure whether to pray to the Jewish God or the Catholic God?

"I prayed to God," she answers simply. "Don't we all pray to God?"

But was there conflict between the two theologies?

"I said the Shamah, which is the holiest of the Jewish Prayers: 'Hear, O Israel, the Lord our God, the Lord is one.' And that's exactly what it is. So, during the day, I was a Catholic girl; at night I became a little Jewish girl, but I prayed to God."

She heard rumors about what was happening to other Jewish children – of the camps and the gas chambers.

"Miss Harar said they burned children. To me, that was a made-up thing. Personally, I didn't believe it."

After the war was all over and Kitty was reunited with her parents, she remembers having to deal with guilt.

"Why didn't the Gestapo knock in the door where my parents were? Why did he save them? I mean, they came so close to being taken.

"There's a reason why we survived, but in the beginning, I was just too happy to be free.

"Then the guilt set in. 'Why me and not all my girlfriends? I actually picked fights with Germans. I'm ashamed to say that, but it's true."

When talking to God now, what does Kitty say?

"I thank God for helping us," she says. "I do that all the time."

I certainly understand Kitty's guilt and confusion. I experienced the same thing.

My mother tried to get papers for me. She actually had me baptized. But we needed the baptismal certificate that proved I was a good little Catholic.

However, the nun at the convent to which she took me refused to issue the precious document, regardless of whether the priest had baptized me. Her excuse was that I had Jewish head form and bone structure – and that Nazi officials would never believe any document that said I was Catholic.

That was ridiculous – as I looked entirely German. I believe the nun was just too scared to try to help us. Perhaps she suspected something or believed that the Nazis were watching. I don't know. I do remember how my mother was irked and disappointed.

From Holocaust to Hallelujah

Even as a small boy, I felt guilty that my mother was suffering this terrible persecution because I was a little Jew.

What I did not know was that my father and were still alive because of her sacrifice. In Berlin, Jews married to non-Jews were among the very last to be deported to the death camps.

Thousands of Jewish children survived through similar sacrifices. Risking their lives, nuns in Catholic convents throughout German-occupied Poland took in Jewish youngsters. Belgian Catholics hid hundreds of children in homes, schools and orphanages.

French Protestant townspeople in and around Le Chambon-sur-Lignon sheltered several thousand Jewish children.

In Albania and Yugoslavia, some Muslim families concealed youngsters. In Denmark, the king announced that if Danish Jews were to wear the yellow star, then he would, too – and so would all Danes. As the Nazis plotted what to do, the people of Denmark evacuated virtually every Jew in the country to safety in neutral Sweden.

But for those of us left behind Nazi lines, many learned to master non-Jewish prayers and rituals in order to keep our Jewish identities hidden from even their closest friends.

Many Jewish youngsters – particularly

those scrambling to stay alive in the streets and burned-out buildings – sought out baptismal certificates with other children's names on them. Such documents were a gift of life – declaring the lie that the Jewish child was instead a Catholic refugee. But it meant denying who and what we were.

Renée Roth-Hanno, author of *Touch Wood: A Girlhood in Occupied France* and its sequel, *Safe Harbors,* has described her childhood turmoil:

"The very first time I experienced faith – a connection with a world beyond my daily one – was in a Catholic convent in Normandy on a mild, early spring day in 1943. I was 11. Paris had been bombed and I hadn't heard from my parents who were hiding in the French capital."

She writes that there was no doubt in her mind that her mother and father were dead, if not from the Allied bombing, then because they had been arrested.

One day, sitting in the convent's garden, she remember, "I was determined to keep my sad thoughts from my two younger sisters. I had settled at the foot of the statue of the Virgin Mary. I thought, she is a mother, isn't she?

After all, of all people, Mary, as a Jewish woman, "would know how it feels to be afraid, to feel lonely. And for a brief moment, it seemed as if she were stretching her arms out for me – a little Jewish girl.

"After the stormy times we had experienced, it was easy enough to bask in the warm and welcoming atmosphere provided by the nuns.

"Eagerly, I set out to put into practice what my sisters and I were being taught in the Catholic school we attended: performing my daily good deed, saying grace before meals, and participating in prayers and songs in a church that embraced us totally.

"How I admired the nuns' selflessness and brave spirit – their risking their lives by taking us in, their scouring the countryside for food in those times of severe rationing.

"They were always respectful of our differences, ushering us into church through the side door so we wouldn't have to genuflect in front of the altar. Yet they were mindful that we blend in. Only when the Germans invaded our town were we secretly baptized to complete our disguise."

Baptism was not easy, she remembers. As the oldest, she felt responsible for her younger sisters. She felt that allowing them and herself to be baptized was a betrayal and that things would never be the same again.

"I had gone to bed one evening an ordinary, innocent 8-year-old, barely knowledgeable about her Jewish faith, and I woke up the next day, forced to flee my home.

"But I could not stop it. I began to sleep walk and to suffer from attacks of breathlessness, so severe that I feared I would die. And I had nightmares that we would go to Heaven without our parents.

"The truth is I had been terribly hurt and scarred as a Jew. I had been startled by the open display of hatred around me in Paris. I was branded as a Jew: compelled to wear the Star of David, banned from movies, cafes and parks, denied a radio and subjected to curfews.

"In the Catholic religion, at least, God is kinder to women, I thought. He made Mary the mother of Jesus, and little Thérèse of Lisieux a saint! The nuns were not afraid of Him – they were married to Him!

"Still, I couldn't trust Him.

"What if He were the same God Jews prayed to and feared, He who couldn't care less about the plight of the Jews – even little children."

I understand her torment.

I felt that same bitterness and anger. Where was the Almighty Creator of the Universe? Why didn't He stop this madness? Why didn't He rescue His chosen people?

"As hidden children," writes Dr. Nechama

Tec, "religion assumed an important place in our lives.

Today, Tec is a senior research fellow at the Miles Lerman Center for the Study of Jewish Resistance at the U.S. Holocaust Memorial Museum in Washington, D.C., and the author of *Dry Tears: The Story of a Lost Childhood.*

"We knew that being Jewish had deprived us of our right to live," he writes. "Being Jewish meant something bad, something for which we could be killed. Being Christian meant being protected.

"The difference between being Christian and being Jewish hinged on different kinds of gods.

"A God that could not even protect His children did not seem very trustworthy. Undoubtedly, the extent to which we followed this kind of reasoning depended on many factors: our age, our Christian protectors and whether we had contact with our parents or with other Jews.

"We were disappointed in our God. We felt abandoned by Him. Yet, we needed consolation from a God, from a religion. Comforted by a new God who promised us acceptance and safety, we were in fact ready for that God.

"By saving us, this new God protected us from evil, and so we equated Him with goodness.

"Many who were old enough to realize what was happening welcomed Catholicism. Those who were very young embraced it blindly. From the perspective of the Jewish child, baptism and Catholicism were positive forces. Each shielded them from danger. Each offered a feeling of security and comfort.

"If being Jewish meant danger, disapproval, something one could be killed for, why would a child want it?

"We were suspended in two worlds: the Christian and the Jewish. Some of us could not reconcile the two. Still others took a definite step toward Christianity or Judaism."

Not me.

I had no particular need of God.

As a street child hiding in the dump, scavenging in the garbage, running from Hitler Youth, I did not look to Him for my daily bread.

He was nowhere to be seen as I stumbled about in the valleys of the shadow of death. He had left us at the mercy of the Nazis when my mother, my father and I needed His protection and safety.

So, what good was He?

I wasn't particularly angry with Him.

I just didn't see Him anywhere.

Chapter Twelve

By the summer of 1944, Berlin was flooded with refugees arriving by the thousands from the war zones. People fled by train, truck, horse cart or on foot, carrying minimal belongings, often without any papers.

The dreaded Russian Army was rolling forward into Germany. Nazi propaganda on the radio about the cruelty of the approaching enemy was frightening to say the least.

I was eight years old in 1944 and somewhat callous to the terror all around me. It was all that I had ever known. I did not miss happy family vacations to the beach because I could not even imagine such a thing.

I did not feel mistreated because I could not attend school. The dump was my school and my playground. The other children there did not talk about themselves. Some were from extremely poor families that had always scavenged from the dump.

Others were Jews who had been through unspeakable horrors in which they lost all their relatives as well as any papers or other belongings. They often made up non-Jewish names and personal histories to tell at the refugee community kitchens, where, looking hungry and exhausted, a shivering child could get a bowl of soup and even food coupons.

Or they would stop at a church-run charity and get second-rate clothing or a bed that night in the refugee shelter.

Jewish kids had to be incredibly street-wise – never tipping their hand. If soup kitchen workers might begin asking questions, the kids knew to pour out a sob story, complete with false names and fake details – always hiding their Jewishness.

Someone would say: "What? You lived in Hamburg! Where was your house?"

"On Wojtiewa Street," the little street

hustler would respond, hesitantly.

"So did my cousin Josefa! What number?"

The street child would mumble some story or claim to have forgotten the details during the craziness of the past few months. The stranger would nod sympathetically and say that Josefa lived next to the cemetery, down from the big Lutheran school.

The next time, the little street hustler would add cousin Josefa, the cemetery and school to the story. Or if someone asked whether he knew the Kowalzkie family, his answer would be evasive, but the Kowalzkies would be his neighbors whenever he told the story again.

If at a loss for details, street kids could always shed a few dramatic tears – and all questioning would usually cease.

Before they sat down to eat, the Jewish street kids knew to recite "Our Fathers" and "Hail Marys" as if they had been saying them forever.

I remember one such kid teaching me how to do the sign of the cross – never with the left hand, always up, down, left, right – and advising me solemnly to get in the habit of doing it automatically whenever I walked by a church or a street shrine or if I saw a cross.

If I used a public restroom, my mother instilled in me that I had to hide my Jewish circumcision behind my hands so others could not see. Jewish boys dared not risk taking showers at the shelters, since they could never count on being alone. Being discovered as circumcised was the surest, deadliest giveaway that you were a Jew.

Gradually, things got worse and worse.

Jews were ordered to stay inside their marked houses for 24 hours a day. Marauding Hitler Youth units, comprised mostly of 12- to 15-year-old hooligans, were armed with pistols and old rifles.

Allied bombings intensified. British and American planes destroyed entire city blocks, leaving roads and streetcar lines in ruins.

Every refugee location was guarded by Nazis. Papers were closely scrutinized and people were dragged away when there was the slightest suspicion of false documents.

How much longer could our family's luck last? Three different times our home took direct hits from Allied bombs. Each time, miraculously, we were not there.

Three times our family had to start over again with nothing after our home was destroyed. I remember once when the house in which we had been staying was reduced to a crater – a hole in the ground. It was difficult to even find our street or recognize it when we got there. Everything was on fire all around us and our apartment simply did not exist anymore. There was nothing to save, nothing to salvage.

Everywhere, there were burning vehicles and carts pushed by refugees, some pulled by animals such as horses, goats and large dogs.

Kids my age clamored through the blown-out windows of devastated buildings to scavenge for food. It had to be done quickly before anyone returned – if they were still alive. Sometimes there were terrible things inside, charred bodies, scattered body parts – pieces of arms and legs, whole families burned to death.

Toward the last, there were lots of bodies on the street, too, and in doorways. Army deserters and suspected Jews were shot on the spot and left there. When cold weather came, the abandoned corpses froze, so there was a constant supply of dead bodies bearing valuable documents, weapons, army and Nazi uniforms, shoes and boots.

Whenever there was an air raid, we rushed into the nearest cellar or basement and waited tensely, listening to the bombs fall. I remember strangers screaming because they couldn't stand it anymore, knowing the next could kill us all.

As the Allied armies approached, the

shelters became increasingly overcrowded with hurt and distraught people shouting, crying and praying as explosion after explosion ripped through the city. People would stumble in, dazed and horribly burned.

In all the smoke and dust, it became difficult to breathe, much less help anyone.

When a raid was over everyone would dig in the rubble for survivors. We kids would carry messages since very few phones still worked.

Always, there was always the danger of another air raid. In fact in the last few weeks before the Russians arrived, we practically lived in the shelter. We could hear the gunfire of the Russian army as the fighting drew ever nearer.

I heard stories about young Jews stealing uniforms and pretending to be Nazis. As an eight-year-old, I could understand their thinking: "What a brilliant idea! Why can't I do that?" I just had to steal the necessary clothing and a few documents.

But I never carried out any such plans. It was a tantalizing temptation. I could be dressed and even armed like a little Nazi. Why not? *We were already pretending to be Christians.* What was the difference with masquerading as a Hitler Youth?

Dressed up as little Nazi hoodlums, I could have gone into a church without fear – because the priests, like anybody else, were terrified of the brutal little Hitler Youth. The clergymen would have given me their own meal – a piece of bread or sausage or hot soup.

But then, again, churches were dangerous, because the Nazi gangs regularly searched churches for Jews.

Yet as a street-wise eight-year-old, I nurtured the lingering, tantalizing prospect of pretending to be a Hitler Youth and going into one of their houses overflowing with food and offering free shelter for the night. Such houses were set up all over the city in abandoned homes, shelters and basements – full of food, weapons, ammunition and loot.

Every day, the challenges to survive became harder and harder for my parents. Temperatures dropped below zero early in the winter of 1944.

Sleeping under rubble, many of the kids at the dump would try to cover themselves with an old overcoat or a blanket, but everybody was perpetually cold and very hungry. The little food we could find was never enough. No longer did rich people discard much of anything.

Many kids would go for a day or two

without anything to eat – and I did, too.

After a while, the hunger becomes less painful and the gut-wrenching stomach cramps ease. It always helped to gnaw on a dry piece of bread, or on a piece of leather just to satisfy my craving to chew on something. Death lurked around every corner, all the time.

We were bombed 24 times between November 1943 and March 1944. Sporadic hits continued until Berlin was captured by the Russian army in April 1945. By that time, the city had been reduced to 98 million cubic yards of rubble.

Over 2,000 tons of bombs had been dropped. Half of the city's bridges were destroyed and the underground railway tunnels were flooded.

There was no gas, electricity or water in the central portion of the city. The pre-war population of 4.3 million had been reduced to 2.8 million, as people fled to the countryside. Some 1.5 million people became homeless when their homes were bombed.

One out of seven of the buildings destroyed in Germany by the Allied bombing were in Berlin. Out of a quarter-million buildings in Berlin, more than 50,000 had been destroyed and 23,000 severely damaged.

There were so many historic buildings

destroyed that Berliners jokingly referred to the American and British air raids as Baedecker Bombing since it appeared that pilots were using Baedecker travel guide books to target famous landmarks.

What the British and Americans started, the Russians finished. The final battle for the city began in April 1945 when the Soviets launched a massive offensive designed to totally annihilate any opposition. It was a brutal fight – house-to-house, street-by-street – with no quarter given on either side.

The agony of the battle ended with the surrender of Germany on May 7, 1945. The city was in ruins, its population wandering the rubble-filled streets searching for food and shelter.

I've heard terrible stories about the Russians and how they treated the people of Berlin.

Again, God protected my family. The Russian soldiers who took over our neighborhood loved children. They doted on us.

By then we were living in a house and the Russian major in charge of our blocks decided to make his headquarters there. Our family had to move to the basement.

But, incredibly, we did not mind so much. The Nazi terror was over.

No longer did we fear being beaten in the street or dragged away to our deaths just because we were Jewish.

Chapter Thirteen

The Russian soldiers who lived in our house were Mongolians and had never been in a city before. I remember coming home and finding my mother mopping up the kitchen. Two of the soldiers had pulled the faucets over the kitchen sink out of the wall.

They thought the faucets were magic – and intended to take them home and stick them in their house so that they could have water flowing out of the wall, too.

I remember vividly as a nine-year-old

getting to eat with them in their mess tent – and being given wonderful, delicious food, complete with meat and sweets. It was the first time I'd ever seen an orange or a banana.

At first, it made me very sick. My stomach could not handle rich food. I had never eaten anything like it before.

Nor was my experience unique. All across Europe, soldiers liberating the death camps had to stop giving the inmates anything but soup and cooked vegetables at first.

Colonel Gerald Draper, a British military officer, recalled, "Men and women clad in rags, and barely able to move from starvation and typhus lay in their straw bunks in every state of filth and degradation. The dead and dying could not be distinguished. Men and women collapsed as they walked and fell dead."

British battle-weary soldiers familiar with the horrors of war were shocked when they stumbled onto Bergen-Belsen concentration camp.

"The inmates had lost all self-respect, were degraded morally to the level of beasts," wrote one soldier. "Their clothes were in rags, teaming with lice, and both inside and outside the huts was an almost continuous carpet of dead bodies, human excreta, rags and filth."

Medical teams were sent to save those who could be saved, but even as they were surrounded with kindness, care and food, it was not enough.

Hundreds died as a result of the richness of their rescuers' army rations. Not being used to such food, their digestive systems couldn't cope. Some were so deteriorated that there was nothing that could be done to save them. British doctors would mark a red cross on the foreheads of those who they thought had any possibility of surviving.

Another British soldier, Peter Combs, sent the following account of the conditions at Bergen-Belsen in a letter to his wife:

"The sight of these affects one profoundly, for while there is still life and movement, we are interested in their salvation mentally and physically.

"The conditions in which these people live are appalling. One has to take a tour around and see their faces, their slow staggering gait and feeble movements.

"The state of their minds is plainly written on their faces, as starvation has reduced their bodies to skeletons. The fact is that all these were once clean-living and sane and certainly not the type to do harm to the Nazis. They are Jews and are dying now at the rate of 300 a day."

Bergen-Belsen survivor Fania Fenelon wrote, "A new life breathed in the camp. Jeeps,

From Holocaust to Hallelujah

command cars and trucks drove around among the barracks. Khaki uniforms abounded, the marvelously substantial material of their battle dress mingling with the rags of the deportees.

"Our liberators were well fed and bursting with health and they moved among our skeletal silhouettes like a surge of life.

"We felt an absurd desire to touch them. They called to one another, whistled cheerfully, then suddenly fell silent, faced with eyes too large, or too intense a gaze. How alive they were, they walked quickly, they ran, they leapt.

"All of these movements were so easy for them, while a single one of them would have taken away our last breath of life. These men seemed not to know that one can live in slow motion, that energy was something you saved."

On the same day that the British entered Bergen-Belsen, American troops entered yet another camp at Nordhausen, where hundreds of slave laborers were found in conditions the United States signal corps recorded as "almost unrecognizable as human."

Soldiers listened in horror as prisoners recounted stories of atrocities. Journalist Robert Weltsch reported:

"The Jewish people have suffered more

than any other people. Only a remnant lives. All of them tell the same horror stories. It would take an entire book to describe these people, their types, their fates, the condition in which one finds them.

"Among them are intellectuals, simple village people, Lithuanian truckers, women, and young people who arrived in the ghettos at the age of 10 or 12 and then went into the concentration camps.

"The old German Jewry no longer exist, all the well-known people have vanished. The synagogues and institutions are destroyed. Germany Jewry has vanished."

The Jews who survived suddenly found themselves faced with perplexing questions. Where now?

For them to go back to Poland, Hungary, Germany made no sense, nor did they want to go. The streets were now empty of Jews and it was a world without Jews.

One survivor describes his liberation as the "beginning of something unknown, disturbing, painful. I knew that all my loved ones at home and at school were dead. At age 16, I felt lost.

"Who was I? What should I do? Where should I go? Where could I find a place called home?"

For us, it would mean returning to a town that had not raised a hand to save us – which had watched and done nothing as my grandparents were dragged away to their deaths.

However, we could not return for other reasons. Schloppe had been returned to Poland, which was occupied by the Russians. My father was concerned that the Soviets were entrenching themselves in all the countries they had "liberated."

Since our house was in what was becoming the Russian sector of Berlin, we gathered our belongings and quietly slipped away, moving to an apartment in the British sector.

So by the summer of 1945, a new part of my life began. I started to learn English. All the Jewish kids were so undernourished that the new civilian authority that became the West German government figured that before they could send us to school, it was necessary to fatten us up a little bit.

Also, there was concern about the little Jewish survivors. I certainly didn't realize it at the time, but we had some emotional and spiritual scars that are difficult to explain.

We might have just been little children, but we had just spent our formative years hiding from people who hated us, escaping from

Hitler Youth who wanted to kill us, and evading the Gestapo who were intent on tracking down our families and exterminating our entire race.

It was one thing to be safe now, after all those years of persecution. It was quite another thing to actually believe it.

It may be hard to understand, but to spend your childhood hiding in a city dump and knowing that you could disappear just like so many of your playmates had, could be enough to give anybody nightmares.

I didn't think I had as serious a problem as some. Some of the kids were bitter and angry.

I was kind of happy-go-lucky. Yes, I had anger. Yes, I harbored resentment. But I was ready to move on – and to believe the officials who fed us and nurtured us and told us everything was going to be OK.

How could I be so easy going about it all? After all, I had just lived through the Holocaust.

I believe it was because my mother was always confident that we were going to survive. She never gave up hope, even when things were impossible.

The new, democratic German government took all the Jewish children and sent them to farms all around Germany.

In September of 1945, I was sent to a little

farm in the southern part of Germany. I was small for my age due to years of hunger. But I was street-wise and sharp beyond my nine years.

The farm family had two children and school had just started, so I went to classes with them even though I didn't enroll. It was a big one-room schoolhouse where all the farm children went.

To go to school and to get back home they had an enormous plow-horse. All three of us would sit on it and ride to school.

Then during school, they had little lean-to shelters on the side of the building where we hitch up our horses. Kids' fathers would bring a bail of hay and buckets of oats. There was a box in each stall where they would put their feed.

At night you would come back home and have a normal family life.

An unusual thing about the farms was that the farmhouses were usually one big building. On one end were the living quarters and on the other end were the stables.

So the family and the cows and the pigs and the horses were just separated by a wall. The funny thing was that at night we could hear, "Snap, snap, snap" where the little mouse traps are snapping and catching the mice.

There were quite a few mice. Every now

and again you would open up a drawer and out would come a mouse. They would chew in from the other side of the wall.

That was an experience. I had a great time.

I got to go out into the field where they were harvesting the hay. We would roll around in the hay. After they brought all the hay to the barn they would pile it all up in the barn.

We would go up into the loft and jump off into the hay and then run up the ladder and see how fast we could do it again.

So we really had a great time. Except for my brief visit to my mother's parents during the war, it really was the first time in my life when my mind was set on playing instead of just surviving. I stayed there three or four months.

I arrived home just before Christmas 1945.

There, I got a terrible surprise.

Chapter Fourteen

My father was gone.

Our family had survived the Holocaust. We had escaped the Nazis. We had survived the Red Army. We had slipped out of what would become Communist East Germany.

But once the terrible ordeal was over, my father decided he didn't want to be a family man anymore. He didn't want to be a husband.

He didn't want to be a father.

He wanted no more of us.

He moved out.

As a boy about to turn ten years old, I was

stunned and hurt, then increasingly angry.

I sided totally with my mother – furious that my father would desert us after all we'd been through. It turned out that he had been unfaithful to us for years. My mother had known about it, but had always shielded me from any hint of his infidelity and the hurt of her personal heartbreak.

My father moved in with a girlfriend – and proceeded to forget all about us. It was as if we had never been a part of his life.

For seven long, dark years, my mother could have just walked away from the Holocaust since she was not Jewish.

She could have gone to the Gestapo, said, "Take him away," and my father would have been removed to Auschwitz or Treblinka or one of those other places of horror and mass murder.

But she had stuck by him – even protected him. Twice, she had actually done the impossible – pleading his case to the Gestapo after he'd been arrested for being Jewish, and talking officials into releasing him. That was unheard of – but she had done it. I had sat there and listened to her do it.

She had suffered the shame of being married against her family's wishes to a cruel man and stuck with him faithfully all through the war.

And now he did this to us.

I know now that she did not run away from the horror because of me. Her love for her little boy kept her in the nightmare.

If she had walked away to safety, I could not have gone with her – and would have been doomed. The next time they arrested my father, they would have taken me, too.

He might have survived a concentration camp, but I would not have. Children under the age of 12 were usually gassed upon arrival – or used for hideous experiments.

She had not known the specifics – none of us did. However, in her mother's heart, she knew she could not leave me.

So, she stayed.

In December 1945, she and I celebrated Christmas alone. I had known there was a Christmas and I knew that people celebrated it, but to me it had meant nothing.

But now, she saw no reason not to celebrate. She had promised my grandfather that I would be raised Jewish – and she had done her best. But now, he was gone.

And so was my father.

So, that Christmas we celebrated for the first time. My mother had saved up and bought me some presents.

In Germany you have St. Nicholas Day on

the 6th of December, but I wasn't home yet then. For Christmas Day my mom tied a number of little pine branches together and we called that a Christmas tree.

Remember, I was ten years old. I thought it was really great.

Then Berlin celebrated the New Year as a free country. Hitler had committed suicide in disgrace. The Russians were far away from us. Our part of the city was peaceful and restoration of the city had began.

I happily joined in.

One of things that had to be done was the streets had to be cleared of debris. You have to understand Berlin had been reduced to almost 100 million cubic yards of rubble.

Half of the city's bridges were destroyed. Some 1.5 million people were homeless. Out of a total of 245,000 buildings in pre-war Berlin, it is estimated that about a fifth had been destroyed and half again severely damaged. Sometimes it was difficult to tell where a street had been.

We kids were enlisted in the rebuilding effort. Before school each day, we would work and then a few hours, too, in the evening after classes.

What could a ten-year-old do to rebuild Berlin? All the bricks had to be gathered. Then we had to take the old mortar off and stack

them neatly in the open doorways.
   A ten-year-old could do that – and I pitched in. It was actually fun.
   All the bricks that had been in the streets from bombed-out houses were cleaned up and stacked in neat piles. We kids would take some of the bricks out and make forts. Some were very elaborate with rooms and halls that led to other rooms. We could play there all day – without worrying about anything.
   Meanwhile, the adults had other tasks. The windows of the bottom floors had to look nice and the streets had to be repaired from the damage done by the bombs and tanks. The Americans gave away sand and cement. We used it to fix the broken streets and sidewalks. There were no official work crews or anything.
   Within four months, Berlin began to look like a city again.
   But there was a deep emptiness.
   As I approached my eleventh birthday, I began to question things. I wondered about God. I would think about how the Jews did not accept me since my mother was Catholic and the Catholics would not accept me because I supposedly looked Jewish.
   And the Nazis had wanted to kill me.
   The emptiness in my soul grew. I would sit and wonder:
   Why had all this been allowed to happen?

Chapter Fifteen

It had been my father's stubborn determination to stay in his native Germany that had thrust our family into the horror of the Holocaust – even when my Uncle Max could see that we needed to escape to America.

If we had listened to Uncle Max, my grandparents would not have been murdered. We would have not have had to suffer through years of persecution.

My mother stayed through the Holocaust because of my father. Now that he had deserted us, there was no reason to remain. She did not want me to grow up as a German.

I was growing tall and turning into a young man. In school, I learned English and quickly caught up with all the other kids – although I had missed kindergarten through the fourth grade.

In what seems a blur, I became a teenager – and a happy one at that. I loved being a part of the rebuilding of Berlin and the new, democratic Germany.

However, my mother saw no reason to remain in a country that had turned its back on us. She didn't like being near my father and his new life. She didn't like the constant reminders of a failed marriage – for which she had sacrificed so much. She didn't want me around him – as he began to get into such things as horse track gambling ... which was really exciting to a young teen wanting the approval of his dad.

So, when as a goodwill gesture the new West German government gave one-way tickets to any Jew who had suffered Nazi persecution, we headed to America.

I remember after our 11-day crossing and the ship reaching New York harbor. I didn't know anything about the Statue of Liberty and could not imagine why people were suddenly shouting and running to the railing on the port side. I had made friends with some American college students who were snapping photos of themselves and other passengers as the lady with the lamp passed by.

I do remember my excitement when I recognized the tall Manhattan skyline I had seen in pictures. There were so many! And none of them were charred by bombs or fire. I wondered whether everybody's houses in New York City were hundreds of stories high and whether we would be living in one.

My Uncle Max had become a U.S. citizen and was our sponsor. However, we stayed with my godparents, the Gotthilfs. Two days after we arrived, I was enrolled in school. Mrs. Gotthilf took me down and enrolled me.

She said that if I didn't go to school I wouldn't learn any English and I might as well learn it there.

I had learned some English in Germany, but it was the Queen's English, British-style. On the ship over, I had discovered to my dismay that Americans spoke a different type altogether and I couldn't understand any of it.

So I went to school and when they made out my schedule for the year, they put me in a Spanish class.

That was crazy because I couldn't even speak their kind of English. Since Spanish is a phonetic language, I did OK as far as reading and writing and spelling, but I didn't know what I was saying.

I had to translate everything from Spanish into English because that was how the class was run and then from English to German so I could understand it, then back to English and from English back to Spanish.

But I did learn American-style English.

And I discovered girls.

In a nearby woods, there was a family with two children. Their girl's name was Shirley. She was in the same grade as I was. She took me under her wing.

She made sure I got on the right busses and went to the right classes and everything.

So we became really good friends.

My other salvation came in the form of two other German boys and an English boy who started school the same time I did.

The Germans had been in America for five months, but they had stayed home and didn't learn any English. The four of us formed an alliance. We stuck together and hung out together because we all had similar problems.

I did well as far as math and science, but in English and social studies and American history, I had a lot to learn. Most of the teachers there were very helpful and patient with me, especially my speech teacher, Mrs. Kuser.

From Holocaust to Hallelujah

She helped me with my sentence structure and paragraphs. If I had to name any teacher over the years who was the greatest help, it would be her.

On the other hand there was a 70-year-old teacher who owned half of the school property. I guess they couldn't fire her.

She really hated Germans. She must have lost some family members in the war or something. She would always make derogatory remarks about Germany and Nazis.

At first, I didn't understand what she was saying, but then when I started understanding, I would get into little arguments with her every now and then.

The absurdity, of course, was that I had just spent most of my life escaping Germans. Now, I was branded a German by a woman who hated them.

Every day, I ended up in the principal's office. It got where the principal would just say, "Have a seat" and I would sit there until the bell rang. Then the principal would say, "OK, go on to your next class."

He didn't want to hear anymore about what I had to say or what I did or didn't do.

We three Germans and the English kid joined the school's soccer team. Almost immediately, there was animosity among the team against us. For one thing, we were foreigners. Then there was the fact that we loved soccer and were quite good at it. We had all played before and knew the game much better than the Americans.

As a result, the girls paid extra attention to us and the other boys of the team didn't like that at all. So when we got on the soccer field they wouldn't pass the ball to us and when we got the ball, they would try to take it away from us.

The coach got real upset about the whole thing, so he told us, "When you get the ball just keep it and pass it between yourselves and cut them out of playing. They'll learn their lesson."

Well, they did.

We all started playing as a team. We did really well. We took three state championships – a phenomenal feat since ours was a tiny little school that had to compete against big city schools.

My aunt and uncle had a chicken farm, so I had to work really hard. I had to get up at 5 in the morning and feed and water all their chickens. Then I had to shower and get ready for school so that at 7:30 I could go out and meet the bus.

That wasn't so bad in the fall, but in the winter when there was snow, I had to dig out a path to the road. It was a tough job.

But in the process, I became an American. *And an agnostic.*

I didn't mind if there was a God. He hadn't done anything for me although I was supposedly one of His "chosen people."

But was I? Jewish boys are supposed to have bar mitzvahs when they turn 13. I didn't since my mother had given up on her promise to raise me Jewish. And there was a deep resentment in my heart against Christians. I thought they didn't want me either. They had refused to give me a baptismal certificate when I needed one to stay alive – even after my mother had me baptized.

So, I didn't figure I owed God anything. His people certainly didn't seem to care anything about me. In fact, I began to find them amusing.

When the Nazis had kept me from going to school, my mother had taught me to read from her family Bible. As a result, I knew Scripture. I could argue Bible history and prophecy.

So any Christian at school who tried to witness to me had his hands full.

I knew the Bible better than any of them.

Chapter Sixteen

What proof did any of them have that Jesus was the Messiah? Most of them would just stare at me blankly.

They had no proof. The idea had never occurred to them. So, I would help them out. I'd point out that if they had studied their Christian history at all, they'd know that there have been lots of false Messiahs before and after Jesus. Two of the most prominent were Bar Kochba and Shabbetai Zevi.

Bar Kochba led a revolt against Rome

perhaps 100 years before the time of Jesus. Thousands of Jews were killed when the Romans stormed their stronghold and ended the revolt.

Zevi drew a lot of attention in 17th-century Europe. But when he was captured in 1666 by the Sultan of Turkey, he converted to Islam rather than face death – somewhat negating his claims to be the Son of God.

Arguing with Christians became one of my favorite pastimes. I did it all the time. They would invite me to their Bible studies or home groups or youth meetings and I would argue and confuse them until they were totally frustrated. I found that amusing.

They didn't even know what they believed.

And so, I spent much of the 1950s as an argumentative, sarcastic, agnostic Jewish Holocaust survivor rejected by fellow Jews and alienated from Christians who wanted to brag that they had "converted" me.

Furthermore, I wanted to get out of rural New Jersey. I hadn't survived the Nazis just to become a chicken farmer. It might be good enough for my aunt and uncle, but I wanted out.

My mother sensed my discontent. After my high school graduation, I went to work for my Uncle Max in nearby Trenton, New Jersey, for about a year. But he was different than I remembered. He had a wife and family now – and wasn't the young German who had been my babysitter in my earliest years.

One day on a whim, I stopped at the armed services recruiting office. The Army told me they would teach me how to fight and to shoot and go on maneuvers.

I figured I didn't have to join the Army to do all that. I could just get drafted and then I would only be in for two years instead of four.

Then, I went to the Marines. They said what a great service they had.

The would teach me to shoot and become a marksman and I would get all the good duties, such as guarding the White House in Washington, D.C., and the Tomb of the Unknown Soldier.

I thought, well, I am gun-shy, so I don't want to spend too much time around guns. Secondly I couldn't see any great joy in standing around and guarding buildings. So, I went to the Navy and they said that I could travel the world and be out at sea for eight or nine months of the year.

I hadn't enjoyed my journey from Germany to America on a ship very much. I knew I didn't want to be on a ship for months at a time.

Then I went to the Air Force.

They said they would teach me a skill and my enlistment time would basically be an 8-to-5 job. So, I thought, that sounds good.

The recruiter said, "Why don't you go on our bus going to Hoboken and you can take your physical? We'll transport you down there and we'll transport you back. We'll pay for your lunch and give you money for the time you miss at work.

"If you pass your physical, then you'll be good for three months and any time you want, you can say you want to get in and you'll be in."

I thought, "Why not?"

I went down to Hoboken for their physical examination and tests and interviews. At the end of the day we all went to this big room.

They shut the door and a major stood in front of the room and talked to us. He said it was time for us to be sworn in.

I said to the sergeant standing in front of the door, "Hey, I'm not supposed to get sworn in."

He said, "Shhh."

And so everybody lifted up their right hand.

I didn't lift mine.

Everyone said they'd swear allegiance to the flag and to the Constitution of the United

States and faithfully serve in the Air Force for their term of duty.

I didn't.

I got out and told the colonel outside the door that I wasn't supposed to get sworn in and he said, "Well, were you in room such and such?"

I said, "Yes, but I wasn't supposed to get sworn in."

He said, "Well you are sworn in."

I said, "I wasn't supposed to. I was only supposed to get a physical."

He said, "Well, there's nothing I can do about it."

This was the 30th of December and New Year's was coming up. I didn't want to be in the service. On the way out, they gave us all our meal tickets and reimbursement checks and a three-day pass and said we had to report back on the third of January to go to basic training.

So, you can imagine the joy when I got home and told my mom that I was in the Air Force and was going to basic training in three days.

She gasped, "What happened?" After all, I was not even a U.S. citizen yet. We had begun our paperwork, but we had another two years before citizenship could be granted.

Three days later, I boarded a bus and was

on my way to Air Force boot camp.

Talk about a new part of my life starting! This was completely different from anything I had ever experienced in my whole life.

After boot camp, I was sent to Denver where I was trained to be a photographer, something I quickly began to love. I enjoyed every aspect of it – taking pictures, working in the dark room – working on cameras.

I was a natural.

Sundays were always a problem. Everybody went to chapel. I let everybody know that I was Jewish. That was only half-true, of course. I was half-Jewish, raised with many of the traditions, but no bar-mitzvah. No Jew considered me truly Jewish.

My friend Joe was Catholic – and supposedly I was also Catholic, baptized anyway. Yet, of course, I wasn't.

We went go to services because there were free doughnuts and coffee if you would sit there and get preached at.

They would tell us all about Jesus and all about Christianity and I finally got tired of hearing about it. One day, the preacher was telling us that Jesus was lying over this chasm and unless we accepted Him we would fall down and go to Hell.

I got tired of hearing this, so I asked the

guy, "Is Jesus a normal-size person?"

He said, "Yes."

I said, "Well, if a normal person can lie across the chasm, then I can jump across it."

He stared at me in surprise.

I grew increasingly obnoxious toward Christians. They had turned me down when I was a desperate little kid. They had been willing to let me die.

Deep down I had a real animosity toward them – more than I realized. I would do anything I could to upset them. I could be really nasty and hateful as they tried to preach to me.

Joe would also get really angry when they told him that all Catholics were going to go to hell because they were not doing things right.

We got pretty tired of it, but it was free coffee and doughnuts, so we kept going. They also had potluck meals where everyone would bring food and all the service people would get to eat free. They also had little shows and even dances afterward.

I didn't miss even one of them. I'm not really a dancer, so would just sit there.

But one night, there was a girl sitting alone across the room, so Joe and I were talking about her. Joe, said, "I bet you won't go over there and ask her for a dance."

I made up some excuse and the other guys heard me.

They double-dared me. I couldn't let them shame me, so I went over and asked her if she would like to dance. I remember it like yesterday.

She smiled like an angel and softly said "Sure."

I was in heaven.

After stepping on her toes for a dance or two, I talked to her and found out that she was a hostess for the dance.

For the longest time, we just talked.

On the way back to the base, all the guys let me know they were impressed. So was I. She liked me. Talking to her filled some aching hole in my very being. I felt complete when I was there with her.

The next time we went, she was there again.

Her name was Mary.

I got to talking to her and after the dance we went down to a local coffee shop and got a soda. We talked some more.

I don't even remember what we talked about. It didn't matter. Just being with her was everything I had ever dreamed of.

We made a date for the next Saturday.

I somehow made it through the longest

week of my life. That Saturday Mary and I went to the park and a museum and we walked all over the place.

We came back and I let her off at her house.

The next week we had another date.

Some time after that, she confessed that she owned a car, but she didn't want me to like her just because of that. *It could not have mattered less to me.*

She told me about her life. When she was in high school, her mother had been killed by a truck in an accident. She had been on her own ever since then.

I told her a little about my life. I couldn't tell her everything – because who could possibly believe what I'd been through? Most people had heard a little about the liberation of the concentration camps, and had kept up with the Nuremburg trials when most of the top Nazis were convicted of crimes against humanity – and hanged.

But that was far away in another world.

Then I learned more about her – and her story was just as incredible. She had been abandoned as a baby, left at an orphanage. It was the height of the Great Depression and often families who couldn't take care of all their kids would give up one or two – particularly a newborn who had a good chance of being adopted.

Sure enough, she was placed with childless parents who loved her dearly and adopted her as their own, but when she was very little, her father vanished and was never heard from again. She didn't know if he had been killed when he went out of state to try to find work or what. But, when her mother was killed, she genuinely was all alone. She was living with Jay and Isabel Rhynard when I met her. She took me home to meet them and we became really good friends. I began to spend a great deal of time over at their house.

Mary and I went on quite a few dates to museums and movies and walks in the park. But looming in my mind was the reality that I was about to end photography school. Soon, I would get my orders.

I would be posted somewhere – maybe thousands of miles away from Mary. I couldn't stand the idea of living without her.

I asked her if she would marry me.
She said that she would.
When I told my friends, they all thought I was crazy. They said, "You just met her and you don't know anything about her."

That wasn't true. I knew everything about her that I needed to know. *I knew that I loved her.*

When Mary told her friends that she

wanted to marry me, they all thought she was crazy. They said it wouldn't last three months.

I didn't have any money. I made $150 a month, which was not enough for a nice ring.

But it turned out that Mary had been engaged to someone else before she met me. He had given her a ring, but when they broke up, she got to keep it.

Since I was so poor, it served as our engagement ring.

We were happy.

And that was enough.

Chapter Seventeen

I took a month's leave to get married, the day after I graduated, June 20, 1955, from the Air Force photography school.

Just as I got everything packed up and told all of my buddies goodbye, they grabbed me and strapped me to my bunk. I couldn't get out. Laughing, they left me there tied up. I spent all morning trying to get free.

They might have thought it was a great joke, but I was frantic. *What was Mary thinking?*

I finally got loose and rushed to her house hours late. I told her what had happened. She thought it was funny. *I did not.*

Our plan was to drive south through the mountains into the state of New Mexico where we would be wed. We packed up Mary's car and off we went to Las Vegas, New Mexico.

It's a beautiful old town with a strong Spanish heritage from when the area was part of Mexico, before New Mexico became a part of the United States.

We went to the courthouse, but the county clerk said that since I was only 19 years old, I needed permission from my parents.

I called my mother in New Jersey and told her I was in New Mexico and needed her to tell the county clerk that I had her permission to get married.

My mother exclaimed, "What?!?"

You have to understand that I am not a very good letter-writer. This was the first time that my mother had heard a word about Mary.

I tried to explain and tell how we had been dating and that I loved Mary very much.

My mother listened.

Then, she said. "You need to come home. I need to meet this girl. I will give you no such permission to run off and get married somewhere in the desert without your family! Plus, you can't get married! You're only a teenager!"

From Holocaust to Hallelujah

I hung up pretty embarrassed.

Somebody in the clerk's office said that in Cleveland, New Mexico, there was a justice of the peace who spoke very little English and would probably let us get married without permission.

We drove to tiny Cleveland and passed a hotel with a guy sitting in front with a big, red beard. I said, "Excuse me, do you know how to get to the courthouse?"

He said, "Sure! You drive down this way and turn right and turn left and turn right and left."

So we went on, but I hadn't understood the directions. We came to a big intersection and I asked somebody on the corner which way we were supposed to go.

The driver in the car behind us leaned his head out the window and called out that we needed to turn left.

When we got to the next corner, I looked around and started to ask directions again, but the driver in that same car was still behind us and said we should turn right. And we did.

We got to the courthouse and went in, but the county clerk was not there. They said she was at a movie. We found out which movie and set out to find her.

When we went back to our car, we could

From Holocaust to Hallelujah

not believe our eyes. Someone had decorated it by writing "Just married," and had tied tin cans to the bumper. Rice had been thrown all over everywhere inside.

Mary and I looked at each other in astonishment. We drove over to the movie theater.

We found the county clerk and she made out the forms for us and gave us a marriage certificate. We went over to the justice of the peace, and sure enough, he spoke hardly any English, just Spanish. His wife was our witness and she spoke absolutely no English.

The other witness was their cousin who owned the drugstore. The justice of the peace began talking in Spanish too fast for me to understand anything and we didn't know what he was saying. Then, he signed the marriage certificate.

We were married!

We drove to our witness's drugstore and both of us had a big ice cream soda. That was our wedding reception. Our witness made us pay for our ice cream.

Then we checked into the hotel. We had to show them our wedding license. Because I was still small for my age, I looked like I was 16 years old. Nobody believed that we were married, so everywhere we went we had to show our wedding license.

We decided to go to a Chinese restaurant for our wedding dinner. We sat down and in came the guy with the red beard who had been sitting on the hotel porch when we first arrived.

"Congratulations," he said.

It turned out that he and some friends had been the ones who put the "Just Married" on our car and the cans.

He said we just looked like we were going to get married and when we asked directions to the courthouse and the county clerk, everybody in town knew it. They thought they would have some fun and mystify us.

Well, they did!

We spent two and a half weeks traveling around New Mexico and Arizona for our honeymoon. We visited the Painted Desert and the Petrified Forest. We even drove down to El Paso and crossed over into Mexico for the day.

We wanted to see a bull fight, but we both felt uneasy being outside of the United States since I wasn't an American citizen and there could be a problem getting back across the border.

I only had my Air Force identification card.

When we got to the border I just flashed my ID card and they said go ahead.

From Holocaust to Hallelujah

We were relieved since that could have turned out to be a harrowing situation.

On our way back to Denver, we were driving through the desert and our marriage certificate flew out of the car. It was a convertible.

I had to chase that marriage certificate across the desert. If we had lost it, we would've been in a pickle. In those days, they didn't let you stay in a motel just by saying that you were "Mr. and Mrs. Jones." You had to have proof.

When we got back to Denver, I received my orders. I was to report to Wiesbaden Air Force Base.

In Germany.

The Air Force had done extensive background checks on me and decided that as a native German with absolutely no Nazi ties, I was valuable to them.

Mary was approved to join me in June, but God had a special surprise for us. During our honeymoon, she had become pregnant with our son, Roger.

The Air Force let her come immediately.

Our son was born at Wiesbaden. We didn't know anybody except the airmen I worked with, so shortly after Mary came home from the hospital, the guys startled us both with a surprise baby shower – although none of them really know how to go about it. They had a cake, Coca-Cola for everybody ... and a luxury baby buggy.

    We were incredibly happy.

Except for one thing.

Chapter Eighteen

I kept up my war with Christians.

I delighted in antagonizing them.

Wherever I was stationed, Mary and I went to services at the Jewish chapel on base – but not that regularly.

Often the rabbi chaplain would say "Oh, Mr. and Mrs. Lewin, it is so nice to see you! You've been here so long and you never come to temple!"

Everyone would look at us. It was embarrassing.

We also made friends with Christians, but

I made sure everyone knew I was Jewish.

They were always inviting us to Bible studies and prayer groups. They wanted to convert me but I always found out that the Christians didn't know anything about what they believed.

They only knew a little about their particular church's doctrine, but they didn't know the Bible. I got a kick out of starting arguments and stirring up dissention.

When they invited me, thinking they were going to convert me, I would go and start arguments. I would make the girls cry and the men glare at me.

I liked to see these Christians struggle.

I kept at it and, incredibly, we continued to get invited more and more. When we were stationed at Travis Air Force Base in California, some friends offered to pay our way to a weeklong Christian couples' camp in Redwoods, California.

They said, "Hey, why don't you and Mary come. We will pay your tuition. Just take your tent and we will have a nice time."

I couldn't turn down something free.

They split us all up into groups of a dozen people or so. Among the special speakers was renowned Christian author Agnes Sanford.

I was in a group that was led by a lady

FROM HOLOCAUST TO HALLELUJAH

from Apple Valley, California.

We were supposed to introduce ourselves. Everyone said I am so and so from such and such. I am a deacon or a pastor or a Sunday school teacher and I go to such and such a church.

When it got to me, I said, "I am Dan Lewin and someone paid my way here so I came and I don't believe any of this stuff. I am Jewish and I think it's a bunch of baloney."

I was ready for a good argument. But the unusual happened. Instead of striking back, they said, "Oh, nice to have you here. We are glad you came. We understand why you feel the way you do." Then they went on to the next person.

I was stunned.

Another guy in the group said he had epilepsy and that he used to work for a phone company. He said, "I'm George. I'm not a believer, either, but my wife said that I had to come so that you guys would pray for me and heal me."

The leader of the group said, "Oh that's great." Then they went on to the next person.

Every time we had a discussion, I made my usual derogatory, argumentative comments.

Each time, they just smiled and said, "Oh,

we are so glad to have you here. You bring so much to the group."

No one would argue with me.

One day they said, "Let's pray for George so he can be delivered from epilepsy."

Everyone agreed. The leader of our group asked me to kneel down in front of George and hold his feet down. We were outside under the trees sitting in folding chairs.

George had keys in his pocket. When they started putting their hands on him, he got really nervous and started shaking. As I grasped his ankles, I could hear the keys rattling on the metal chair.

They began praying. "Oh Lord, heal him."

I was impressed at first, but then it began to get old as they went on and on and on. I thought it was funny and tried not to laugh out loud. I just chuckled to myself. These people were like children. They had no idea of the real world.

Then all of the sudden, as I held his ankles and tried not to laugh out loud, it was as if electricity shot through George. It was as if I had grabbed a loose power cord.

George stopped shaking.

I thought they had killed him. He stopped moving and there I was holding his feet. I didn't even want to look up. I knew there was going to be big trouble.

Then somebody exclaimed, "Praise the Lord!"

Somebody else asked George, "How do you feel?"

He said, "Great! Look, I am not shaking anymore."

Everyone said, "Thank you Jesus."

The lady from Apple Valley said, "Well, Dan, is this the first healing you've ever witnessed?"

Stunned, I answered that it certainly was.

"Jesus is the one who did it for George," she said. "And he did it so you could see the power of God."

I was stunned.

They prayed for me to receive Jesus and the Holy Spirit.

But I wasn't so sure.

George and I had a long talk. I told him I wanted to see if he stayed healed.

The next day one of the camp's speakers, Frank Laubach, dropped by our group. Everyone told him about George and me. He told us that God loved granting prayer requests.

He turned to me and asked if I had any prayer requests. I was startled and I said, "Well, it is hot here. I think we could use some rain."

So, they all prayed for rain – for God to send some refreshment for the ground. Then we talked about my being a Jew and how Christians really love Jews and they are special to them.

I was startled to hear that. I could just remember the nun refusing to give my mother a baptismal certificate. I could hear all the people who had preached at me that Jews had killed Jesus and that unless I repented, I was going straight to a special place in hell.

Then it started to rain.

It rained and rained and pretty soon I thought our tent was going to float away.

It just kept raining.

The next morning, being the skeptic that I was, I waded out to the car and drove to the nearest gas station.

I asked if the attendant was a local man.

He was.

I asked if it rained like this very often.

He laughed. "Rain?" he exclaimed. "It *never* rains in the summer and when it does, it doesn't last long."

In fact, he said he last time he could remember rain like this was in 1904.

I got into the car and drove back to camp.

I was convinced.

No one needed to tell me anything about

FROM HOLOCAUST TO HALLELUJAH

Jesus after that. I began to talk to Him myself.
And I *surrendered.*
I asked Him into my heart.
I was filled with an ecstasy that I still cannot describe. Maybe it's what they call being "born again." Maybe it's what the Bible describes as being a "new creature" or experiencing the "renewal of your mind."
I just knew it was real.
The next morning, they told us all to draw a picture or write a story about the best thing we liked about the camp. I drew a picture of the cross and a lot of people going to it. I am not very artistic, but it looked really good.
When we arrived back home, I was so excited and I sought out Mary's pastor. I told him I was going into the ministry.
He knew me and winced.
"Don't worry about it," he advised me. "Don't let it affect you to much. It will blow over soon. Don't rush into anything too soon. You will settle down."

He was wrong. I started attending every meeting that the church had. I went to all the services and even the youth groups.
One day, the youth had a special speaker and we found out that whoever had agreed to bring the refreshments had forgotten, so there wasn't any snack.

Someone volunteered to go buy something,

The speaker said that maybe this is God's way of teaching us faith.

"Let's just pray for refreshments," he said. "God will provide them if we are supposed to have them. If not, then we will be all right."

We prayed and then went on with the meeting. There was a knock on the door and there was a guy there nobody recognized. He seemed embarrassed.

"I noticed all these cars here," he said. "I was supposed to take a delivery to a wedding party, but there was a mistake and the store sent me with a birthday cake and punch."

He said instead of throwing it away, perhaps he could give it to us. "Maybe you all can use it instead," he said.

I was not astonished at all. I had begun to see God in a completely different way. He was not a mean, demanding ogre sending terrible things our way. No, he was a loving, doting Father who grieved over the terrible darkness that His beloved children wandered in.

He yearned for them to step into the light.

I had learned that God was not about arguments. He was not about nitpicking over doctrine.

He was about love.

I had been saved by His grace.

My sins were forgiven.

And I didn't have to quit being Dan Lewin. God had created me like I was. He had allowed me to go through a terrible test – an unbelievably nightmarish childhood.

Although I never wanted to see war again, the Air Force sent me on two tours of duty in Vietnam as a combat photographer.

I became known as the "Good Luck Charm" since nothing bad seemed to happen if I was nearby. For example, it was the day *after* I finished a photo assignment at a Green Beret camp in the jungle that they were overrun by the Viet Cong – and everybody was killed.

Another assignment sent me out with a combat unit that was ambushed ... but none of us received a scratch.

While waiting in line at the Saigon airport to see Mary, a bomb blew up in the luggage of the Airman in front of me. I wasn't there since I had gone to get a cup of coffee at the airport restaurant.

I met and photographed such notables as comedian Bob Hope, actor Raymond Burr and even the King of Thailand. I covered everything from SeaBees to Navy SEALS, Army Special Forces and Marine combat units.

I can tell you with certainty that luck had

nothing to do with it. God's hand was on me continually.

God brought me through it.

For a reason.

Chapter Nineteen

It would be ridiculous for me to claim that my life has been all roses and sunshine since those days so long ago. But I can tell you this for certain: *God loves me. He always has.* Some of His children are woefully imperfect ... just as I still am today.

Back in Germany a fearful nun had no idea the terrible impact she had on a little boy for whom she refused to make a baptismal certificate. But I have probably made similar mistakes. *And I have forgiven her.*

Let me tell you something else that may be difficult to accept.

I have forgiven Adolf Hitler.

I have forgiven the Hitler Youth who chased me and pulled down my pants to see if I was a little Jew – and would have bragged about killing me if I was not so good at getting away.

I have forgiven the Nazis who sent my grandparents to the gas chamber. I have forgiven my father for deserting us after my mother sacrificed so much for us.

Instead of deep bitterness, I have peace.

I frequently meet other Holocaust survivors and I understand why some of them are so consumed with revenge. Some have devoted their lives to tracking down the Nazi leaders who escaped. I understand, but I know that I cannot live in the past.

I have believed for years that my personal story must be told. The Nazi Holocaust against the Jews of Europe must be remembered – and Christians must understand that it was not just a Jewish tragedy.

As I have tried to write this story, I have faced a serious challenge. I don't remember so many things. Entire years are a blank.

As I have tried to record what happened to me, details of incidents will come back. But the truth is that my once-tortured memory has been healed. God has touched me in a special way.

He allowed me to forgive the unforgivable

From Holocaust to Hallelujah

... and to forget the unforgettable.

I have been allowed to move on. Mary and I are retired now from my photography shop in Hot Springs, Arkansas. One thing has not changed. I still look forward to running into people who want to argue about Christianity.

Argumentative Jews are my special love. I delight in striking up a conversation with young know-it-alls and seeing if they will argue with me. I don't always tell them that I am Jewish or that I am a Holocaust survivor – one of the 100,000 or so legendary "hidden children" who evaded the Nazis – or that I did it right under Hitler's nose, right in the middle of Berlin ... playing in the dump!

Instead, I try to show them God's love. That's what convinced me. I pray silently that He will reveal Himself to them in some special way, just as he did with George and rain and a birthday cake.

I could fill a book with the arguments that I hear. *But the answer to them all is really simple.* God is no abstract concept. He is not a mysterious, distant being that stands afar off, aloof and disinterested, posing riddles. From the first, He has loved mankind and still yearns to commune with His greatest creation.

When He delivered Israel from slavery in Egypt during the time of Moses, He demonstrated – just as He has throughout history, as well as today – that He will provide daily for us. He expects only our love in return.

He wants each of us to seek Him – individually. In the musical play and movie *Fiddler on the Roof,* Tevye the Milkman had it right when he spent so much of his day talking with God, seeking His help in this and that.

There are great and terrible forces of evil which despise our Almighty Creator. The only way God can be hurt is by separating His beloved children from Him.

The bottom line is very simple.

God loves us. He loves *you.*

He promised us he would send a Messiah and did just that about 2,000 years ago. He yearns for us all to accept that Deliverer and the special gift that Jesus offers: *grace,* God's willingness to forgive everything we've ever done.

A famous Christian author, David DuPlessis, once wrote that God has no grandchildren. *How true!* No one is a Christian simply by being born into a Christian family. It doesn't matter whether your mother is a wonderful person or if your grandfather was a great theologian. You do not inherit God's grace because of your bloodline. No, salvation is a gift that each of us has to accept one-on-one, just you and the Creator.

No one can force you to become a Christian. If you recite a written prayer at gunpoint, that does not make you a Christian. Being baptized at the convent didn't do a thing for me. Reading a creed, walking down an aisle at a revival meeting, or kneeling at a mourner's bench are not enough to make you a Christian.

The Apostle John writes in the first chapter of his Gospel, verses 11 and 12, that the gift of becoming God's child is freely given when we freely receive Jesus, believing He is who He said He is – God's Son – and accepting the gift that our Father offers each of us – eternal life in the presence of the Creator of All.

Have you done that yet? *I have.*

As a result today, I have a peace that defies all human understanding.

I know it only comes from the Father.

He loves me. He has looked out for me ever since I was born – and my many experiences have made me who I am today.

Yes, my life was difficult at times. Even after becoming a Christian, I have endured difficulties. But, I am no longer alone.

I am no longer at odds with my Creator.

He is my friend. He delights in providing for me. Oh, yes, there have been deep disappointments.

I returned to Berlin and found my father. He had not changed – in fact was worse in some ways. Just before he died, his latest new wife took everything, so I inherited nothing.

But God blessed me, far more than I would have received from my father's estate.

My deepest hurt is that I am afraid that my dad died without Jesus. I mourn that deeply – for I would so love to spend eternity with him. He was a brilliant man.

I believe he listened to God's nudging – particularly when he saved our lives by taking us to Berlin where we hid in plain sight.

Today, I am a father and so proud of my own children. The firstborn, Roger, is married to Lynda, a wonderful schoolteacher, and they are presently doing mission work in Africa.

Our twins, Trevor and Tracy, were born in 1967 when I was stationed at Vandenberg Air Force Base in California. Trevor works with the deaf and helped start a Christian outreach to the deaf in Hot Springs.

Tracy graduated from the University of Arkansas with a Master's degree in mechanical engineering. He had his own computer business and now works for one of the world's largest computer companies.

The most important thing is that our children know Jesus. I know I will spend eternity with them when that time comes.

My mother died in 1989. Mary and I had brought her to Hot Springs to live near us. She didn't attend church with us – she had her own issues with Christians and religion in general.

I talked with her many times about the Lord and, I think I inherited some of my ability to argue from her. She listened and would tell me she agreed that Jesus was a good man with some good ideas. However, she was not ready to accept Him at the level I had. *I think she'd been hurt too deeply by some of His children.*

One night when she was very ill, a German couple from our church came by to pray for her. She had been in a coma for several days. When they prayed for her, she woke up and greeted everybody. She was completely lucid.

She listened as they talked with her about her need to accept Jesus. She smiled. She had heard this so many times from me. But this time, she prayed with them, asked the Lord to forgive her sins, accepted Him into her heart, then went to sleep peacefully.

The next morning, she was gone.

Although it hurt terribly to lose her, I have such joy knowing that, praise God, He had her in His hand all the time. I know I will get to spend eternity with the wonderful, complex, loving woman who protected me at such enormous risk to herself. She was willing to sacrifice everything for her little boy.

She loved me.

And taught me to love in return.

Postscript

I said in the beginning that nothing in our lives just happens.

Whatever occurs, God uses to teach us. He teaches us how to cope. Our ability to cope is much of what makes us who and what we are.

A childhood of terrible persecution taught me to withstand and not complain. To roll with the punches that life gives us. If the Holocaust had not occurred, Israel might never have been restored as a nation – and I might never have come to America.

No matter how bad things seem there is always someone who is worse off who would want to trade situations with you.

I have learned to thank God for every day and every experience that he gives me. Each event has formed a tapestry, a beautiful patchwork quilt that has been my life.

I am so thankful that I was allowed to come to America and spend these all these years as an American. I was not pleased at the time that my mother dragged me here as a teen. But God was in control.

I am especially thankful that He allowed me to learn that love is free. The love I received from my uncle, my grandparents, my mother and my wonderful wife sustained me – and prepared me to be able to accept God's love.

God works in our lives constantly. When things aren't going well, we must never forget that He is at work. He has not promised us a bed of roses, but He does teach us how to live with the thorns – and to take a deep breath and smell His beautiful roses.

Let me leave you with this: If you want to be truly happy, set in your heart that you will daily ask God how you can help others. Focusing on others, you won't have time to worry about yourself or sit around feeling sorry for yourself because, like some of us, you have really had a rough time.

That is why I can now shout "Hallelujah, Praise the Lord!"

Bitterness and self-pity don't work.

I know.